40 SEASONAL MEALS, 100 RECIPES, AND LOADS OF TIPS
AND STRATEGIES TO MAKE WEEKNIGHT DINNERS WORK

Reclaim the family dinner! In *Feeding a Family*, nutritionist and mom Sarah Waldman lays out all the tools you need to break out of the mealtime rut and turn dinner into a nutritionally fulfilling and happy occasion—despite busy schedules, long work days, and picky eaters. Through forty complete meals, you'll discover hearty dinners the whole family will love, including:

- A meal for using up the best summer garden produce: Make-ahead Zucchini, Beef, and Haloumi Cheese Skewers with Chimichurri Sauce paired with Tomato, Peach, and Red Onion Panzanella and Lemon-Blackberry Custard

- A cozy and comforting dinner for a frenzied fall day: Creamy Tomato and Spinach Soup with Grilled Cheese Croutons and Pear Pie in Cornmeal Crust

- The perfect meal for the busiest night of the week: Slow Cooker Indian Butter Chicken with Sweet Peas and Lemon-Pecan Shortbread Cookies

- A warming (and fun) winter meal: One-pot Slurpee Noodle Bowls with simple Chocolate, Peanut Butter, and Date Truffles for dessert

- Sunday suppers for when you have a bit more time to play in the kitchen, such as Homemade Pasta with Heirloom Tomato Sauce and Pavlova with Blueberries

With suggestions for including older kids in mealtime prep, tips for feeding baby, and ideas for extending ingredients for "tomorrow's dinner," *Feeding a Family* is a playbook that includes the whole family.

FEEDING *a* FAMILY

Sarah Waldman
photographs by Elizabeth Cecil

FEEDING *a* FAMILY

A Real-Life Plan for
Making Dinner Work

ROOST BOOKS

BOULDER

2017

Roost Books

An imprint of Shambhala Publications, Inc.

4720 Walnut Street

Boulder, Colorado 80301

roostbooks.com

9 8 7 6 5 4 3 2 1

First Edition

Printed in the United States of America

⊗This edition is printed on acid-free paper that meets
the American National Standards Institute Z39.48
Standard.

♻ Shambhala Publications makes every effort to print
on recycled paper. For more information please visit
www.shambhala.com.

Distributed in the United States by Penguin Random
House LLC and in Canada by Random House of Canada Ltd

Designed by Daniel Urban-Brown

Library of Congress Cataloging-in-Publication Data

Names: Waldman, Sarah, author. | Cecil, Elizabeth,
photographer.

Title: Feeding a family: a real-life plan for making
dinner work / Sarah Waldman; photographs by
Elizabeth Cecil.

Description: First edition. | Boulder: Roost Books,
an imprint of Shambhala Publications, Inc., [2017] |
Includes index.

Identifiers: LCCN 2016012234 | ISBN 9781611803099
(hardcover: alk. paper)

Subjects: LCSH: Cooking, American. | Seasonal cook-
ing. | Dinners and dining. | LCGFT: Cookbooks.

Classification: LCC TX715 .W176 2017 | DDC
641.5973—dc23 LC record available at https://lccn.loc
.gov/2016012234

for Dylan & Gray—the loves of my life

Contents

Introduction

In the summer of 2008, I became obsessed with food. Not only food, but what was happening to food in America (spoiler alert—it wasn't and still isn't good). I read books by Marion Nestle, Michael Pollan, Mark Bittman, Sally Fallon, Walter Willett, and Ellyn Satter. I felt equally depressed and enlightened. Processed and packaged foods were trying to take over our country, and I became determined to help stop the epidemic of low-quality food appearing on family dinner tables.

I enrolled in the Institute of Integrative Nutrition, had a baby, then another, and began counseling people on how to navigate the modern food industry by building a diet made up of whole, seasonal foods. Today, as a busy mom of two young boys, my life still revolves around food, but in a completely different way. My reality is a hungry family that depends on me (mostly) to provide them with nutritious, home-cooked meals. And guess what—it's hard! Between work, school, and life I continually have to dig *really* deep to figure out how to pull this dinner thing off, night after night. My challenges are that one kid will devour a hamburger at twelve months while the other does not eat meat, we live nowhere near a big fancy grocery store, and we have a tight food budget.

The struggle to feed a family is real, and I know I'm not alone. Daily, friends will rush up to me in the school parking lot or library and ask, "What's for dinner?" They ask not because I'm an expert but because I might have an idea for something new, or I might just tell them it's okay to make egg sandwiches. Everyone wants to know how to make dinner work because when it works it is a great source of pride, connection, and light at the end of a long day. But when it doesn't work, dinnertime is depleting, depressing, and so unbelievably stressful.

But here's the thing—we shouldn't add cooking guilt to our already full plate of parental self-blame, especially when feeding our family is such a personal and emotional job. No matter who you are or what your cooking background may be, you can make the time for simple home-cooked dinners. You *can* reclaim dinner for your family.

I'm here to help with this daunting process. Throughout this book I offer guidance, inspiration, and concrete ideas on how to make family dinner work. And there is the food, of course. The recipes included in this book are our family favorites—the meals that have been in our regular rotation for years, as well as recent discoveries that have quickly become staples at our house. There are many recipes in this book that my kids eat weekly, if not daily, like Banana Milk with Flax Seeds (page 43) and Black Bean Quinoa Burgers (page 52). Other dishes that my husband, Nick, or I happen to love (hello, Roasted Green Beans with Scallions, page 206) are entirely aspirational: the boys have never chosen to eat a full bite of them, but I continue to cook and serve these foods, knowing that someday they may catch on.

Each season offers ten dinner menus. Some dinners are one-pot meals, while others have a few sides or even a dessert. I hope the menu-style organization takes the guesswork out of what to serve with what and gives you a good list to start with at the beginning of each season. Although many dinners have desserts, I am not suggesting you make and eat dessert this often. Rather, I'm hoping these simple, wholesome sweets will come in handy when planning a seasonal celebration, special birthday treat (let's try not to bring loads of artificial sugar into schools), or after-school baking project (sanity saved!).

These recipes are for easy, everyday meals, but many of the dinners can be simplified and adapted even further. For example, Creamy Pumpkin Fettuccine (page 73), which calls for spinach fettuccine to be tossed in creamy pumpkin alfredo sauce and then topped with pumpkin seed pesto, is still delicious with just one sauce—creamy or pesto. And Sweet Pea Oven Risotto (page 104) is great with finely chopped asparagus instead of peas. Make the recipes your own by subbing in your family's favorite ingredients and the produce available around your home. Each season also offers a slower Sunday dinner that often involves family participation. These are the kinds of meals that start in the morning, chug along, and end with a messy kitchen and full table.

I have invited four guest families to share their favorite seasonal dinners so you can see what works in other family kitchens. These families are all busy, hardworking, down-to-earth food lovers. You'll also notice that I've included notes throughout the book on how to adapt the dinners to feed an infant (nobody wants to unnecessarily cook the baby a separate meal), recipe tasks kids can do, and ways to transform parts of the meal into a second dinner.

We started documenting our family meals for this book in the winter, so that is where the recipes start. All the cooking, photography, and writing were completed in season, thus the stories and recipes take us through one full year, in real time.

How to Feed a Family

So how exactly do we pull this nightly family dinner thing off—not just getting a meal on the table but actually enjoying it? This section explores the big ideas behind the family meal, from why family dinner is so important to what can be done about "picky eaters." Here, I have outlined my personal inspirations, ideas, and steps for creating a rhythm of home-cooked dinners. These thoughts are organized into bulleted, easy-to-read lists so your precious time is not wasted searching for helpful bits amid lengthy paragraphs. I hope you find nuggets of information here that really resonate with you. I drafted these lists to be photocopied and hung on a fridge, e-mailed between friends, or used to kick off an important family meeting. I still reference many of these reminders on a daily basis and hope that you leave this section energized and inspired.

THE BENEFITS OF FAMILY DINNER

At our core we all know family dinners are a good idea. Maybe it's the memory of a meal decades ago—one where you heard an infamous family story for the first time or watched your infant try, and love, curry chicken. Perhaps it was the meal when you noticed your twelve-year-old son looking like a teenager. Strong memories and emotions are good reasons to eat together, but the facts don't hurt either.

Children embrace the predictability of a nightly family event.

Dinner conversations support and expand children's verbal and reading skills.

Family dinner time is a rare opportunity to share family history and stories.

(continued)

At mealtime, parents and older children model expected social behavior, which helps younger children develop their own social skills.

It is generally agreed that children who eat with parents or siblings at the table eat more nutritious foods during their meal.

Children who participate in regular family meals do better nutritionally, academically, socially, and emotionally. (Ellyn Satter, *Secrets of Feeding a Healthy Family*)

Regular family meals affect children more positively than extracurricular activities, church, tutoring, and music lessons do. (Ellyn Satter, *Secrets of Feeding a Healthy Family*)

Teenagers who eat dinner with their families are less likely to smoke, drink alcohol, and do drugs. (The National Center on Addiction & Substance Abuse at Columbia University)

FAMILY NUTRITION AND SEASONAL WHOLE FOODS

Nutrition information is overwhelming and often confusing. We are bombarded with nutritional messages everywhere, from food packaging (Fiber! No sugar!) to articles in parenting magazines (Try this new superfood!) and meaningful conversations with our pediatricians. Often, the language is hard to understand and the different messages quickly contradict each other. I think we have overcomplicated things. My advice is to simply focus on eating and serving a variety of whole foods—that's it. If the food is in season, cue the fireworks.

Cooking and eating what is growing outside is not a new concept, but the availability of global produce has made us numb to the natural connection between season and plant. Children, however, are naturally aware of the changing seasons (imagine a five-year-old on the first snowy day), and we can take a cue from them. By building our meals with what is growing, we automatically satisfy our cravings and consume foods that our bodies need (think nutrient-dense sweet potatoes in the winter and hydrating melons in the summer). I realize that there are so many rules around eating healthfully, seasonally, and locally that a very simple and natural process has become overly confusing, daunting, and not so fun. I encourage you to ease up on expectations and guilt. Just being aware of what is in season and doing your best to work some of those items into your family's meals is enough. You can always build upon your initial efforts. And remember, nobody is perfect. We treat our boys to blueberry-topped yogurt in February and buy bananas that grow far away from our northern home. In the end, I think a bowl full of blueberries is still better than none—if those berries are from your local farmer or garden, all the better.

It is important to note that every body is different—some people feel their best eating dairy, red meat, or wheat, while others have adverse reactions to these foods. No two bodies need and want the exact same things. Above all else, I hope this information will allow you to step back and look at the big picture.

Before you serve it, ask: *Is this a whole food?* Meaning, can a farmer grow it? Is it a whole or piece of an original food? For example, an apple is whole, but apple juice is not. How long have people been planting, eating, and cooking this food? Generally, the more unprocessed a food is, the more nutrients it contains.

Adults and children should eat a balanced diet made up of whole grains, vegetables, proteins (legumes, nuts, seeds, dairy, meat, poultry, fish, eggs, tofu), fruits, and fats (nuts, seeds, avocado, oils, coconut, lard). Everybody finds his or her own balance between these foods. Use these groups to guide your daily, weekly, and monthly meal planning. You can also use this as a tool for kids to choose the components of meals (just pick a favorite item from a few categories). A quick review of these general categories makes it clear what types of foods your family, child, or self are lacking. In the end, step back and ask yourself: *Did our family meet these requirements over a meal, week, month, or season?*

No one food group has all the nutrients our bodies need, but all the basic food groups combined offer a nutritious diet.

Nutrition directly affects daily energy, mood, temperament, and long-term health for adults and children alike.

Your family's eating attitudes and relationships with food are more important than what they actually eat on any given day. If general attitudes and behaviors are positive, individuals will eat well and get the nutrition they need.

(continued)

Rather than labeling a food as "not bad" (for example, you may think crackers are "not bad" compared to a donut), ask yourself: *What is the nutritional benefit of this food?* This question helps me clarify and focus on foods that have a positive effect on the health of my family and me, and separate out those that are not obviously harmful but do not offer important nutritional benefits either (like those crackers).

When you do order a pizza (or another favorite takeout dinner) after a marathon day, serve it with a bowl of raw, sliced fruit and vegetables and your family's favorite milk or smoothie. This way, everyone will fill up on a variety of foods and not overdo it on takeout.

Locally grown food tastes better, as it is not packed and shipped far distances or picked before it's ripe. It also produces less pollution, due to its short travel time.

Shopping locally keeps your money in your local economy.

When you see a price tag, think of what that food is also "costing" in terms of your health, environment, and the local economy.

Join a CSA (community-supported agriculture) or plant a garden for access to high-quality produce. If a child grows a plant, they are more likely to taste and enjoy it.

Freeze in-season produce for use year-round. Cleaned and chopped produce is best frozen on large baking sheets, then transferred to freezer bags to eliminate big clumps.

Buying in bulk means that you are not spending your money on unnecessary packaging and advertising.

Encourage your favorite and most conveniently located markets to offer more locally grown items.

Find a balance between your budget and your ideals.

Time is the biggest obstacle to the family dinner. But, feeding your family is *really* important, and, I dare say, feeding your family poorly can become dangerous. Adjust your priorities to make the time to prepare a handful of planned dinners every week (maybe three or four), and fill out the rest of the week with quick pantry meals (see page 14).

First, look at your activities and then do some time juggling. What does your family's extracurricular time look like over the week or month? How much is spent on things like baseball practice vs. cooking for yourselves? Block off time on the weekends, early mornings, or evenings, or outsource specific tasks to your partner. Too tired to cook after work? Then don't cook after work! Maybe it is as simple as getting up twenty minutes earlier to get dinner into the slow cooker, moving a radio into the kitchen, or watching your favorite show while prepping on Sunday. No one is asking you to give up things you like, but feeding a family does take thought and time. We need to make meal planning, shopping, and prepping a priority. Our modern culture is trying to convince us that time spent on dinner preparation is wasted time, and that we need to multitask during mealtime to keep up. Not true. What we need is to find ways to make cooking food and eating together fit into our busy lives. It is not a lost cause, but it does require a unified effort.

Aim to cook three or four dinners a week. Fill out the rest of the week with quick pantry dinners (page 14) or leftovers.

Plan your weekly meals as a family by looking through cookbooks and magazines or reviewing a small notebook of favorite recorded meals.

Build and maintain a well-stocked pantry (more on this on page 13). You'll always pick up more groceries than you really need at the store (even with a good list), but if you know your kitchen is full of useful ingredients at all times, you'll be less likely to overbuy.

Clean out the pantry and fridge as often as you can, and while you put weekly groceries away, consolidate containers of the same item, recycle empty containers, toss what is old, and organize the rest.

(continued)

Once a month, shop for pantry items and staples. Once a week, shop for produce. Keep an ongoing shopping list on the fridge organized into two columns: pantry and produce.

All family members can help with supporting jobs, such as quickly organizing the pantry and fridge during grocery unpacking, adding items to a master shopping list, loading and unloading the dishwasher, setting and clearing the table, and emptying the garbage.

Prepping even the smallest thing ahead of time helps—mixing a sauce, filling a pot with water, or arranging vegetables on a roasting tray.

Prepare produce whenever you can before cooking time. Chopping onions, peeling carrots, and washing kale leaves seem like small steps but are a huge help come cooking time.

Cook ahead. Preparing a pot of whole grains, a tray of roasted vegetables, or side dishes that can keep in the fridge makes mealtime all the more organized.

Use some canned and packaged foods. Things like canned beans, whole peeled tomatoes, and low-sodium chicken broth are no-brainers in a busy kitchen.

Invest in machines that help. A basic food processor, blender, and grill pan are all simple time-saving tools in a family kitchen.

Look to your equally busy friends for support. Maybe you gather on Sunday afternoons to cook or shop together. You can also each make a batch of something (pizza dough, soup) and trade to share the wealth.

INVOLVING THE WHOLE FAMILY

The goal is to avoid placing the brunt of family dinner responsibilities (from meal brainstorming to shopping, prepping, cooking, and cleaning) on just one person. If these important roles fall to one family member, that person is going to get burnt out, resentful, or just stop having fun. We are looking for a long-term solution that is sustainable and inclusive of all family members. Dinnertime will be the most successful if everyone takes some ownership and draws pride from the process. And in the long run, what is the worst that could happen by inviting the kids to crack a few eggs or chop the celery? Sure, you may have to choke down a couple of eggshell bites or serve a very "rustic"-looking salad, but there will be no long-term damages.

Hold a family meeting to kick off your dinner project. Talk about why it is going to be so fun and have family members choose jobs, such as recipe selection, shopping help, table setting, picking flowers for the table, calling the family to dinner, making homemade placemats or nametags, and cleaning up by carrying dishes to the sink, sweeping the floor, and loading the dishwasher.

Always invite the kids to help with cooking, but if they don't want to, don't push it.

Follow your children's lead in the kitchen—see what they like to cook and what tasks interest them. Maybe physical work like tearing kale leaves and peeling or chopping vegetables is their thing. Calmer tasks like measuring and mixing or decorating the dinner table appeal to others.

Invest in child-friendly kitchen tools that work for your kids. Tools that are unsafe or frustrating make cooking together stressful. (Hello, nervous hovering parent!) Our boys' favorite kitchen tools are a pizza cutter (to slice bread, tortillas, greens, soft fruit), child-safe knives (for general chopping and slicing), kitchen shears (for trimming fruits and vegetables), and small wooden rolling pins and mixing spoons. We also have a light-but-sturdy kitchen stool, which the boys can move around themselves when they need a boost.

Lead by example. If you are angry and frazzled in the kitchen, it is likely everyone in the house is going to pick up on your feelings. Sad but true. It is best to invite younger kids to help when you are in a good mood and not in a total rush.

Relax. Cooking with little people (or your partner!) is not always smooth sailing. Things spill, more baking powder is added than you had hoped, some of the sliced apples are huge (with seeds hanging off) and others are tiny slivers. This is what family dinner looks like, and it is okay. Overly correcting and imposing rules on kitchen helpers is going to lower their pride and discourage them from helping next time. And yes, your kitchen is going to get messy.

"Picky eaters" is a new phrase that did not exist in our grandparents' time. By picky eaters I am not talking about those who have confirmed food allergies or medical sensitivities; I am talking about kids who can (seemingly) not participate in family meals. I completely understand why and how picky eating habits are formed, because we as busy parents ease up on the expectations of our children's eating. We are exhausted, frustrated, and feel guilty about almost everything. At the start, however, most babies are enthusiastic eaters. In fact, infants often show a pure, open relationship with food. As kids grow up, behaviors, personalities, and opinions are thrown into the mix and things get complicated. The truth is, kids are capable of eating a range of whole foods, and we as parents can be sensitive to their likes and dislikes without catering to every request. Believe it or not, the pressure to eat a variety of whole foods is already within your child—in their desire to grow and to mirror you as a grown-up. The meals your family cooks and serves will become a fact of your child's world, and they will adapt to dinnertime like they do to everything else. It's the period of adaptation that is bumpy.

When I needed help with a picky preschooler, I turned to Ellyn Satter, a family therapist, feeding expert, and the author of a collection of books about nutrition and feeding of children. I found Satter's advice extremely helpful when our oldest son was four and our youngest was one. I was exhausted and had slacked off on our family's eating habits. With renewed determination and energy, we regrouped and dramatically improved our family meals. The following advice is gleaned from Satter's various books and writings, and has helped me and my family stay on track and deal with the issue of pickiness.

Hold a family meeting to discuss the start of new dinner rules or to regroup after noticing changes at mealtime. I find myself calling a family dinner meeting every few months to remind our family of our basic rules.

Phones and other electronic devices are not allowed at the table for any family members.

Arrange food choices on the table and let everyone pick what they like. It's okay if someone chooses only one food, but there should be at least one food item that you know everyone likes. More often than not, our dinnertime spread includes a loaf of whole-wheat bread with butter and a bowl of sliced apples.

Find meals that can be tweaked with toppings or sauces to meet individual preferences, like Kale and Sweet Potato Tacos (page 78) and Noodle Bowls (page 26).

Avoid meals made up of all new ingredients. Children like to see something familiar.

Nobody should be pressured into eating anything they don't like, provided that they say "no, thank you" politely (not "yuck!"). Family members (including adults) can say "that's not my style" or "I don't like the tomatoes" (or other specific ingredient) so it is clear what is a turnoff. It is okay to spit something out after you try it.

Try not to stress out if specific foods are refused (for example, leafy greens or brown rice). Focus on eating those items yourself and offer them again at another meal.

Stay cool. Do your best not to comment on your kids' eating at the dinner table. Serve the food, then watch what people choose, eat, and decline without fanfare.

The kitchen is closed after dinner. If kids choose not to eat dinner, no biggie—they just have to wait until the next meal. Yes, this can be extremely hard in the beginning (I've been in many a "just a banana!!!" life-or-death situations), but if you are consistent and dinner happens at roughly the same time every night, kids will know what to expect and the consequences that come with their choices.

Babies, toddlers, and children can take a long time to eat, as the event is as much about filling their bellies as it is about exploring colors and textures, practicing feeding, and using utensils. Don't rush through dinner; rather, sit tight and go at their pace.

Take care in what you (and other role models) eat, as children are observing you and are very influenced by your choices. Think about your relationship with the "picky" foods. Do you cook, serve, and eat a lot of them?

(continued)

Look at what time you're eating dinner. I slowly discovered (after watching trays and trays of snacks being gobbled up) that our boys are the most hungry and truly ready to eat dinner at 4:30 or 5:00 P.M. each day. This makes sense, as they are home from a long day and are asleep just a couple of hours later. Of course, it is a challenge to have a family meal at this time, but the earlier you serve dinner, the less snacking is necessary and the more hunger (a natural motivator) will kick-start mealtime eating.

Keep perspective. When Gray was an infant, I was really worried that he was eating too many bananas. He wanted a banana with every meal, so naturally I thought I did something wrong and he would never eat foods without a sweet fruit included. I came to realize that if my biggest feeding problem was that my baby really liked bananas, then I had it good. He outgrew the banana phase pretty quickly.

Don't camouflage the "picky" food in a recipe, but instead include it with a favorite food. Hiding healthy foods makes children distrustful and suspicious. I'd rather have my kids know what broccoli looks and tastes like, and not like it, than try to hide the vegetable from them in pancakes and brownies. However, serving something like broccoli in a favorite food (pasta, rice, or soup) is one way to open them up to the food in a familiar way.

If it's not on their plate (or on your dinner table), they can't eat it. I realize how ridiculous this sounds, but it's true. The only way kids can get used to a new food and have the opportunity to try it again is if it is served to them—again and again.

If dessert is a struggle (a bargaining tool, constant request, or nightly argument), start by not making it a reward. Instead, put a sensible serving of dessert at each place when you set the table. Dessert should not be served every night. Sometimes a simple dark chocolate chip is our "dessert," and it goes over very well. Ultimately, sweet treats that are no longer banned become normal foods that can be consumed in normal ways.

Keep Ellyn Satter's golden rule (from *Secrets of Feeding a Healthy Family*) in mind: "You do the feeding and your child does the eating and growing. Parents are responsible for what, when, where of feeding. Children are responsible for how much and whether of eating."

Building a Family Pantry

A well-stocked pantry is a key piece of the dinner puzzle. When staple items are stocked and organized, cooking dinner is faster and shopping trips are less daunting (not to mention that feeling of triumph when I open the pantry to look for a specific ingredient and find it there staring at me!). On those nights when you come home late or don't have a specific dinner planned, a simple meal can be quickly prepared from a well-stocked pantry.

MY PANTRY STAPLES

This master list includes every pantry item you need to cook every dish in this book. I find all these items in our small town market and keep them in my kitchen at all times.

DRIED FRUIT

Dates

Dried Peaches

Raisins

FLOURS

Bread Flour

Buckwheat Flour

Cornmeal

Unbleached All-Purpose Flour

Whole-Wheat All-Purpose Flour

Whole-Wheat Pastry Flour

LEGUMES

Black Beans

Chickpeas

Green Lentils

Red Lentils

MISCELLANEOUS

Arrowroot Powder

Bread Crumbs (panko and regular)

Chicken Broth

Coconut Milk

Diced Tomatoes

Dijon Mustard

(cont.)

Hot Sauce

Miso Paste

Nori

Sriracha

Tomato Paste

Unsweetened Cocoa Powder

Unsweetened Shredded Coconut

Vegetable Broth

Whole Peeled Tomatoes

Worcestershire Sauce

NUTS AND SEEDS

Almond Butter

Almonds (sliced and whole)

Chia Seeds

Flax Seeds

Hazelnuts

Peanuts (dry roasted)

Peanut Butter

Pecans

Pine Nuts

Pumpkin Seeds
(Pepitas)

Sesame Seeds

Tahini

OILS

Canola Oil

Coconut Oil

Extra Virgin Olive Oil

Sesame Oil

PASTAS AND NOODLES

Dried Semolina Pasta

Dried Spinach Pasta

(cont.)

Dried Whole-Wheat
Pasta

Soba Noodles

Udon Noodles

SPICES AND FLAVORINGS

Chili Powder

Cinnamon (ground)

Cumin (ground)

Curry Paste

Curry Powder

Pure Vanilla Extract

Red Pepper Flakes

Turmeric (ground)

SWEETENERS

Agave Nectar

Brown Rice Syrup

Brown Sugar

Cane Sugar

Coconut Sugar

Honey

Maple Syrup (pure)

VINEGARS

Apple Cider Vinegar

Red Wine Vinegar

Rice Vinegar

WHOLE GRAINS

Arborio Rice

Barley

Black Forbidden Rice

Brown Rice

Farro

Long-Grain Rice

Quinoa

Red Bulgur

Sushi Rice

QUICK DINNERS FROM PANTRY AND FRIDGE STAPLES

Remember, dinner does not have to be a life-changing meal every night. Here are our favorite dinners made from pantry and fridge staples. Some of these ideas may not look like "dinner" to you, but I would like to redefine the term. To me, any home-cooked meal—however simple—is a successful dinner.

ROASTED VEGGIE PASTA: Toss cooked pasta with roasted vegetables and tomato sauce or pesto.

BAKED SWEET POTATO BAR: Serve baked sweet potatoes with refried beans, cheese, and other toppings on the side.

EGG SANDWICHES: Layer fried eggs, sliced avocado, tomato, red onion, and cheese on toasted bread.

RICE & BEANS: Cook a pot of rice, stir in a can of drained and rinsed beans, and serve with toppings such as sliced mango, cabbage slaw, ground pork, sour cream, or cheese.

FRUITY BUTTERMILK PANCAKES: Make buttermilk pancake batter and dot with fresh, seasonal fruit before cooking.

PANTRY SOUP: In a large pot, combine a quart or two of chicken stock, drained chickpeas, baby spinach leaves, fresh lemon juice, and leftover rice, tortellini, or shredded chicken. Heat until warm.

KIDNEY BEAN DIP: In a food processor, puree two cans of drained kidney beans with two cups of shredded jack cheese and some pickled jalapeños (to taste). Scoop the dip into a casserole dish and warm it in the oven; serve with pita chips and cut veggies.

GREEN BREAKFAST: Scramble some eggs, stir in finely chopped sautéed greens, and serve with roasted potatoes and bacon.

SAUSAGES & PEPPERS: Grill up local sausages and top them with a quick sauté of colorful peppers and onions. Serve with whatever grain you want to use up.

TACOS OR BURRITOS: Fill small corn or flour tortillas with almost anything, from grilled chicken and avocado to refried beans and scrambled eggs.

SOBA NOODLES & TOFU: Boil soba noodles and toss them with low-sodium soy sauce and sesame oil. In a hot, oiled pan, stir-fry cubed tofu and any vegetables you have on hand. Add the noodles to the pan and toss well.

PARFAITS: In tall glasses, layer whole-milk yogurt, homemade granola, and fresh berries.

QUICK CURRY: Stir a couple of tablespoons of curry paste into a can of full-fat coconut milk. Squirt in some lemon, thin it out with water, and toss in drained chickpeas or leftover chicken—maybe even some frozen peas. Simmer over medium heat until warmed through. Serve with brown rice.

Winter

Winter dinners do so much. They warm us up physically, from the snow and wind, and mentally, from the idea of *five months* of snow and wind. Fierce winter storms often cause the ferries to and from Martha's Vineyard to stop running, and suddenly we find ourselves stranded on an island, or perhaps even stranded inside a small cottage, for days upon end. Desperate times call for desperate measures—another Chocolate, Peanut Butter, and Date Truffle (page 29), anyone? Despite the challenges, winter may be my favorite cooking season. It is about hunkering down, making do with what you have, and eating filling meals before heading off early to bed. The dark afternoons and evenings are long, so it is the perfect time to focus on family participation in the kitchen, whether that involves looking through a cookbook to pick out a new soup or rolling sushi together for a Roasted Root Vegetable Sushi Bar (page 38). But perhaps most important, winter meals soothe sick bodies, tired and weak with runny noses. Working a variety of winter greens, hot broths, and vitamin C–packed citrus into your family's cold-weather diet will help ward off some of the ickiness. Happily, our hardy winter dinners lend themselves to leftovers that taste even better the next day, packed into lunch boxes or transformed into second meals.

Winter Meals

21
PIZZA NIGHT

Kale, Herbed Ricotta, and Local
Sausage Pan Pizza

Fresh Citrus Fruit

25
SLURPEE NOODLE BOWLS

Noodle Bowls

Chocolate, Peanut Butter, and Date Truffles

31
THE ONE-SKILLET WONDERS

Chicken Thighs with Barley, Chard,
and Mushrooms

Cinnamon and Sugar Chickpeas

37
JAPANESE TAKEOUT AT HOME

Roasted Root Vegetable Sushi Bar

Quick Miso Soup

Banana Milk with Flax Seeds

45
A LIGHT AND COLORFUL WINTER MEAL

Gado Gado Salad

Broiled Honey-Vanilla Grapefruits

51
OUR FAVORITE VEGGIE BURGERS

Black Bean Quinoa Burgers

Roasted Carrots with Honey Butter

Quick Citrus–Dark Chocolate Cake

59
THE MORIARTYS' FAMILY MEAL

Chicken Tortilla Soup

Churros with Mexican Chocolate Dipping Sauce

65
KIDS EATING FISH

Cod Cakes with Poached Eggs

Quick Arugula Salad

Slow Cooker Brown Rice Pudding

71
ORANGE AND GREEN PASTA BOWLS

Creamy Pumpkin Fettuccine

Pumpkin Seed Pesto

Roasted Broccolini

77
**WINTER SUNDAY SUPPER
(AND A CAMPFIRE PARTY)**

Kale and Sweet Potato Tacos

Corn Tortillas

Slow Cooker Black Beans

Honey Marshmallows

Pizza Night

KALE, HERBED RICOTTA, AND LOCAL SAUSAGE PAN PIZZA
FRESH CITRUS FRUIT

Our oldest son has never eaten a piece of animal meat. This is going on five-plus years, and I'm curious to see where it ends up. His brother, on the other hand, dove for a spicy pork taco and gobbled it down in a flash just after his first birthday. Needless to say, they have different tastes. Pizza is one of those simple family dinners that pleases us all. We often top half the pie with something most of the family likes and the other half with another thing most of the family likes—I call that even. Don't let this pizza dough intimidate you. It's something you can throw together the night before and leave until dinnertime the next evening. To balance out the hearty pizza, I often slice up a few citrus fruits for a refreshing and simple side. Anything from clementines to blood oranges or grapefruits will do—they all add welcomed winter freshness to our table.

KALE, HERBED RICOTTA, AND LOCAL SAUSAGE PAN PIZZA

makes one 12 by 18-inch pan pizza

Over the past nine years, Nick has been on a quest to master a variety of pizza techniques at home, from a classic Margherita to this "Grandma" pie. He has experimented with different flour varieties, forms of tomato (fresh, canned, sauce), cheeses, and cooking techniques. Happily, his hard work has led us to some darn good home-cooked pizza. If you're feeding a crowd (or love cold pizza as much as we do), simply make two bowls of dough and put the kids in charge of their own pie to have ready for lunch boxes the next day. In the cold months, this dense pan pizza is our favorite. Here, a simple overnight dough (just mix and leave it in the fridge before bed) is topped with creamy ricotta cheese, pork sausage, and kale. As an added bonus, the 500°F oven is a welcome guest in a cold, February kitchen, always taking the edge off the drafts coming up through the floorboards.

KIDS CAN: Little helpers can tear kale leaves from stems, stir the ricotta cheese mixture, and push the pizza dough into the pan.

DOUGH

1 package (2¼ teaspoons) active dry yeast

1½ cups warm water

1 teaspoon kosher salt

3 tablespoons extra virgin olive oil, divided

4 cups unbleached all-purpose flour

PIZZA

1 big bunch kale (about 13 kale leaves)

5 tablespoons extra virgin olive oil, divided

¼ cup water

Kosher salt

1 pound pork sausage (hot or sweet), removed from casings

1 cup whole-milk ricotta cheese

Zest of ½ lemon

Leaves from 2 sprigs fresh thyme, chopped

Leaves from 1 sprig fresh rosemary, chopped

1 cup marinara sauce (your favorite brand or homemade)

---

1. Make the dough the night before your pizza dinner. First, in a large bowl, whisk the yeast into the water until it dissolves. Let the mix stand for 10 minutes (you should see some bubbly foam form on top of the water). Using a wooden spoon, stir in the salt and 2 tablespoons of the olive oil, then add the flour 1 cup at a time, stirring after each addition. Mix everything together and turn the dough out onto a floured countertop. Knead for 5 minutes until

soft and springy. Place the kneaded dough into a clean bowl coated with the remaining tablespoon of olive oil. Cover the bowl with plastic wrap and leave it in the fridge until dinnertime the following day.

2. Take the dough out of the fridge to come to room temperature. When you're ready to make the pizza, set a rack in the lower third of your oven and preheat to 500°F. While the oven heats, slice the kale leaves into thin ribbons. Heat 2 tablespoons of the olive oil in a large skillet over medium heat, add the kale ribbons, water, and a pinch of salt, and sauté for 5 minutes, until the kale is wilted. Transfer the kale to a plate and use the same pan to cook the sausage.

Cook the sausage over medium heat until brown, about 10 minutes, breaking the meat apart with the back of a wooden spoon.

3. While the kale and sausage cook, mix the ricotta in a small bowl with a pinch of salt, the lemon zest, and the chopped thyme and rosemary.

4. To prepare for baking, coat a 12 by 18-inch rimmed baking sheet with the remaining 3 tablespoons of olive oil. Slowly stretch the dough across the pan, pushing it into the corners with your fingers. Top the dough with a layer of tomato sauce, then add the kale, sausage, and small dollops of the flavored ricotta. Bake for 15 minutes. Remove the pizza from the oven, cut it into squares, and serve immediately.

FOR BABY: Finely chop a bit of cooked sausage and kale, then mix it with ¼ cup of plain ricotta cheese. Thin out the mixture with water or milk if it looks too dry. Finely dice some citrus fruits for finger food.

Slurpee Noodle Bowls

NOODLE BOWLS

CHOCOLATE, PEANUT BUTTER, AND DATE TRUFFLES

Like most kids I know, Dylan counts peanut noodles among his favorite meals. After serving up my hundredth batch of peanut noodles, I knew we had to shake things up—at least for my own sake! This meal is inspired by the creamy and salty noodles we all love but with fresh, crisp toppings and a warming broth. After a light meal like Noodle Bowls, one of us will almost always request something rich and sweet for dessert. As this request typically falls right before bedtime, a labor-intensive baking project is not in the cards. However, quick Chocolate, Peanut Butter, and Date Truffles can be made in under ten minutes. The slightly sticky, chocolate-scented dough is ideal for little hands to roll and decorate, creating the perfect, nutritious treat to nibble on with a bedtime story or while being coaxed into a warm bath.

NOODLE BOWLS

serves 4

Don't be turned off by the long list of ingredients—this dinner is really just a dash of this and spritz of that all piled into one simple pot. If your family is not a fan of tofu, simply omit it or replace it with your favorite vegetables or shredded meat. Regular pasta is also a fine replacement for udon noodles if you don't have them on hand.

KIDS CAN: Put older kids in charge of preparing the noodle bowl toppings.

NOODLE BOWLS

2 garlic cloves

1 yellow onion

1-inch piece fresh gingerroot

2 tablespoons canola oil, divided

1 to 2 tablespoons green curry paste

1 teaspoon agave nectar

1 teaspoon sesame oil

½ teaspoon kosher salt

1 teaspoon ground turmeric

5 tablespoons soy sauce

1 package extra-firm tofu, cut into ¼-inch cubes

One 15-ounce can full-fat coconut milk

3 cups chicken broth

8 ounces udon noodles

Juice of 1 lime

1 tablespoon creamy peanut butter

TOPPINGS

1 shallot, minced

½ head purple cabbage, finely shredded

1 lime, sliced

1 cup dry roasted peanuts, chopped

1 cup bean sprouts

1 cup chopped fresh cilantro

Sriracha

---

1. Using a food processor, whiz the garlic, onion, and ginger together until finely minced. In a medium soup pot, heat 1 tablespoon of the canola oil over medium heat. Add the garlic, onion, and ginger mixture and cook until soft and fragrant, about 3 minutes. Add in the curry paste, agave, sesame oil, salt, turmeric, and soy sauce and cook for another 3 minutes, stirring everything together. Add in the tofu and gently toss the cubes to coat them with the flavored mixture. Next, pour in the coconut milk and broth. Bring the soup to a strong simmer, then turn the heat

down to low and let it cook while you prepare the noodles and toppings.

2. Cook the noodles per the package directions (typically 6 minutes in boiling water). Strain the noodles and toss them with the remaining tablespoon of canola oil.

3. Depending on your time, prepare the toppings by hand or use a food processor to shred the cabbage and finely chop the shallot, peanuts, and cilantro in quick batches.

4. Before serving, finish the broth by whisking in the lime juice and peanut butter. Taste the

broth and add more curry paste or soy sauce if need be. To serve, pile the noodles in the bottom of individual soup bowls, top with broth, and then pile on the toppings.

FOR BABY: In a small saucepan, warm a handful of minced tofu and cooked noodles in ½ cup of plain chicken broth.

TOMORROW'S DINNER: STIR-FRY

Shred the remaining half head of purple cabbage and, using a large wok, stir-fry the cabbage, some thinly sliced chicken/pork/tofu, garlic, and fresh ginger in canola oil. Serve over brown rice with any remaining noodle bowl toppings.

CHOCOLATE, PEANUT BUTTER, AND DATE TRUFFLES

makes 20 truffles

Not only are these raw truffles the perfect treat before an early January bedtime, but they also make ideal Valentine's Day "candies" for school friends, teachers, or neighbors. Tailor the recipe for your valentine by choosing a favorite food (salty peanuts in this case) to coat the balls with—anything from toasted shredded coconut to crystallized ginger works. If you're feeling extra ambitious (or have a long, dark afternoon on your hands), make a variety pack with a few different toppings.

KIDS CAN: For some sticky fun, kids can be in charge of pitting the dates and rolling the truffles.

---

2 lightly packed cups pitted dates

½ teaspoon pure vanilla extract

⅓ cup creamy peanut butter

¼ cup unsweetened shredded coconut

2 tablespoons natural cocoa powder

Pinch of kosher salt

⅓ cup dry roasted peanuts, chopped

---

1. Using a food processor, whiz the dates and vanilla together until a sticky paste forms. Add in the peanut butter, coconut, cocoa powder, and salt. Pulse about a dozen times to combine all the ingredients.

2. When you're ready to roll the truffles, put the chopped peanuts in a shallow bowl and turn the truffle dough out onto a clean counter. Using your hands, grab a golf ball–size piece of dough and roll it into a ball. Place the ball into the peanuts and gently roll it around to adhere the nuts. Continue rolling out all the truffles. The finished truffles can be stored in an airtight container at room temperature for a few days, or in the refrigerator for up to 2 weeks. They are best served at room temperature.

FOR BABY: Finely chop a couple of dates and roll the sticky pieces in a sprinkling of coconut.

The One-Skillet Wonders

CHICKEN THIGHS WITH BARLEY, CHARD, AND MUSHROOMS

CINNAMON AND SUGAR CHICKPEAS

Who doesn't love a dinner that involves just tossing everything into one pan? It makes preparing dinner a cinch, and won't add more pots and pans to the already aggressive pile of sink dishes. Often times one-pot meals (I'm thinking women's magazine casseroles here) call for too many cans of processed ingredients, filled with sodium and additives, to be mixed together into an unidentifiable mush. Not here—in this dish, whole grains, leafy greens, tomatoes, and chicken are layered together and popped into the oven. If you have time in the evening, early morning, or during naptime, this skillet can be assembled in five minutes, covered, and left in the fridge, waiting for you. Now go put that time saved on dishes to some good use (with a warming whisky cocktail, perhaps?).

CHICKEN THIGHS WITH BARLEY, CHARD, AND MUSHROOMS

serves 4

When I first came up with this simple one-skillet dinner, I shared it with my sister Anna, knowing it was right up her alley. Later that day, she sent me a picture of her cast iron skillet meal, along with a note: "Toss in a cup of barley with the veggies—it's great." Genius! The liquid from the veggies and chicken plumps up the barley beautifully, and in just forty minutes you have a complete meal ready to go. If mushrooms aren't your thing, or if you are throwing this together in the summer, use halved cherry tomatoes or thinly sliced zucchini rounds instead—both work perfectly.

3 tablespoons olive oil, divided

One 28-ounce can diced tomatoes

1 bunch Swiss chard, leaves removed from stems and torn into small pieces (stems can be saved for soup or stir-fry)

8 ounces white button mushrooms, stemmed and chopped

2 garlic cloves, smashed

2 teaspoons kosher salt, plus more as needed

1 cup barley

1 cup low-sodium chicken broth

4 bone-in, skin-on chicken thighs

Freshly ground black pepper

4 sprigs fresh thyme

1 lemon, sliced

1. Preheat the oven to 425°F. Brush 2 tablespoons of the olive oil across the bottom of a 10-inch cast iron skillet. In a large bowl, toss together the tomatoes, chard, mushrooms, garlic, and 1 teaspoon of the salt. Place half of the vegetable mixture in the bottom of the cast iron skillet, and pour the barley over the top. Add the rest of the vegetable mixture and the chicken broth.

2. Arrange the chicken thighs on top of the veg-

gie and barley layers, pushing them gently into the skillet. Sprinkle the chicken with the remaining teaspoon of salt and a few grinds of pepper, then drizzle the skins with the remaining tablespoon of olive oil. Toss in the thyme and sliced lemon. Transfer the skillet to the oven and roast for 35 to 45 minutes until the skin begins to brown and the barley is tender. If you like extra-crisp skin, put the pan under the broiler for the last few minutes. Serve immediately.

FOR BABY: Mash a small bowl of chicken, barley, and vegetables with the back of a spoon or puree the mixture with an immersion blender.

TOMORROW'S DINNER: SOUP

Create a simple chicken, barley, and vegetable soup. Heat a small pot of chicken or vegetable broth and stir in any leftover diced chicken and vegetable-barley mixture. Simmer over low heat, just to warm it through. Serve with Parmesan cheese and crusty bread.

CINNAMON AND SUGAR CHICKPEAS

serves 4

The mild flavor and creamy texture of chickpeas allow these beans to be easily transformed into a high-protein treat. Here, I toss them with coconut oil, cinnamon, and sugar and sauté them until crisp and golden. Your house will smell as good as they taste.

19 ounces canned chickpeas

2 tablespoons coconut oil

Pinch of kosher salt

3 tablespoons granulated sweetener (coconut sugar, pure cane sugar, or date sugar)

2 teaspoons ground cinnamon

1. Drain and rinse the chickpeas, then dry them on a kitchen towel. If the skins pop off during the drying process, simply discard them.

2. Melt the coconut oil in a medium skillet over medium heat.

3. In a large mixing bowl, stir together the chickpeas, salt, granulated sweetener, cinnamon, and 1 tablespoon of the melted coconut oil (leave the remaining coconut oil in the skillet). Ask your little helper to stir until all the chickpeas are coated.

4. Turn the skillet up to medium-high heat. Toss in the flavored chickpeas and arrange them in a single layer. Let the chickpeas crisp up for about 2 minutes without stirring, then toss them and repeat the crisping/tossing process until they are caramelized and smell delicious, about 2 to 5 minutes more. Cinnamon and Sugar Chickpeas are best eaten warm right out of the pan.

FOR BABY: Smash a few crispy chickpeas with the back of a fork for finger feeding.

Japanese Takeout at Home

ROASTED ROOT VEGETABLE SUSHI BAR

QUICK MISO SOUP

BANANA MILK WITH FLAX SEEDS

I know it is the start of the long, dark season when I find myself turning the car's headlights on while driving home from school. When dinnertime rolls around, the sky is pitch-black and I feel like it could be midnight, despite the rambunctious kids playing nearby. These long evenings need a spark to keep my spirits up. When we lived in a city, the spark was a stroll down to our favorite Thai or Japanese restaurant, but these days that is not an option. Martha's Vineyard's winter food scene is far from diverse (you won't find pho or curry anywhere), so we have to do it ourselves. This sushi bar and miso soup dinner is our best attempt at making a takeout meal of our own. To top it off, I am sharing the boys' most loved one-minute dessert.

ROASTED ROOT VEGETABLE SUSHI BAR

makes 5 to 6 rolls

Meals that encourage family collaboration, like this Roasted Root Vegetable Sushi Bar, rolled along to a little music, help to keep me out of the winter dumps. Our sushi bar allows for family members to build what they like and take charge of their dinner.

P.S.: You only have to cook rice and roast a tray of vegetables!

KIDS CAN: For dinner, kids can peel the root vegetables, mix the sushi rice with vinegar and sugar, and assemble the nori rolls.

FILLINGS	RICE	TO ASSEMBLE
1 sweet potato	2 cups sushi rice	5 to 6 nori sheets
3 carrots	2 cups water	Low-sodium soy sauce
2 parsnips	2 tablespoons rice vinegar	Pickled ginger
2 tablespoons olive oil	2 tablespoons pure cane sugar	Wasabi
2 avocados	1 teaspoon kosher salt	

1. You want to get the vegetables in the oven first, as they take the longest to cook. To save time, you can always peel and slice the root vegetables the night before and store them in a bowl full of cold water in the refrigerator. Preheat the oven to 425°F. Peel the root vegetables and slice them into 3-inch sticks. Toss the vegetable sticks with olive oil and a sprinkling of salt, then arrange them in a single layer on a baking sheet. Roast for 20 minutes, until tender and edges begin to brown.

2. While the veggies roast, prepare the rice. Combine the sushi rice and water in a medium saucepan over high heat. Bring to a boil, uncovered, then reduce the heat to low and cover the pan. Cook the rice for 15 minutes, then remove the pot from the heat and let it stand, covered, for 10 minutes.

3. Whisk together the vinegar, sugar, and salt in a small bowl. Pour the vinegar mixture over the rice and toss with a fork to thoroughly combine.

4. When you are ready to assemble the sushi rolls, pit and slice the avocados. Set up a rolling station with the roasted root vegetables, sliced avocado, sushi rice, nori wrappers, and a small bowl of water close at hand. To roll, cover a nori sheet with a layer of sushi rice, leaving one-quarter of

(continued)

the sheet clear. Next, pile up a horizontal strip of roasted root vegetables and avocado slices in the middle of the sushi rice. To roll, wet the top of the exposed nori sheet, then fold the bottom of the sheet in on itself, tightly rolling it along to the top. Seal and lay the roll on a cutting board. Slice with a wet, sharp knife. Serve the sushi with low-sodium soy sauce, pickled ginger, and wasabi.

FOR BABY: Infants can enjoy a bowl of rice topped with smashed or minced vegetables and sprinkled with bits of nori.

TOMORROW'S DINNER: WINTER TACOS
Double the amount of vegetables you roast for the sushi rolls so that you have leftovers. Tomorrow night, make tacos with black beans, tortillas, roasted root vegetables, and toppings (avocado, sour cream, cheese, lime, and cilantro).

QUICK MISO SOUP

serves 4 to 6

This Quick Miso Soup is a favorite of mine, as it takes only about 15 minutes from pot to bowl and has the deep, earthy flavors I love.

---

6 cups water

½ ounce dried bonito flakes

6 tablespoons miso paste (white or red)

8 ounces firm tofu, cut into ½-inch cubes

¼ cup finely chopped dried wakame seaweed (if it is too brittle to chop with a knife, use kitchen shears instead)

4 scallions, white and light green parts only, thinly sliced, for serving

1 tablespoon sesame seeds, for serving

---

1. Combine the water and bonito flakes in a medium saucepan and bring the mixture to a boil. Turn the heat down to a gentle simmer and cook the broth for 5 minutes. Turn off the heat and let the pot sit for 5 more minutes.

2. Strain the broth through a fine-mesh sieve, discard the bonito flakes, and return the clear broth to the pot over low heat. In a small bowl, whisk together the miso paste and ⅓ cup of the warm broth. Pour the miso mix into the soup, then drop in the tofu cubes, seaweed, and scallions. Cook until the seaweed becomes soft in the soup, about 5 minutes. Serve the miso soup warm, sprinkled with sesame seeds.

BANANA MILK WITH FLAX SEEDS

makes 2 glasses

This recipe is our boys' favorite nightcap (as I write this I can hear a little one-year-old voice requesting "nana milk"). This thick smoothie is blended up in a minute and is full of fragrant winter spice, healthy fats, and fiber. Tailor the banana milk to your infant's stage, choosing from yogurt, almond milk, hemp milk, coconut milk, cow's milk, or even goat's milk.

---

2 ripe bananas

2 cups whole cow's milk (or whatever type of milk you like)

½ teaspoon pure vanilla extract

½ teaspoon ground cinnamon

1 tablespoon flax seeds

OPTIONAL ADD-INS

1 tablespoon unsweetened shredded coconut

1 tablespoon nut or seed butter

2 dates

Small handful of nuts

1 tablespoon unsweetened cocoa powder

---

1. Using a powerful blender, simply blend all the ingredients together until smooth. Pour into two glasses and enjoy. Banana Milk with Flax Seeds is best sipped down right away, as the drink slowly separates.

A Light and Colorful Winter Meal

GADO GADO SALAD

BROILED HONEY-VANILLA GRAPEFRUITS

There comes a point every winter when I start craving fresh, raw foods rather than rich roasts. Maybe my body is looking forward to spring or is telling me to load up on naturally detoxifying raw fruits and vegetables to help ward off an impending cold. Either way, it is always a nice change to enjoy a dinner like this Gado Gado Salad, full of crisp and crunchy carrots and cabbage, followed by a dessert like these Broiled Honey-Vanilla Grapefruits, bursting with tart, coral-pink juices. I pull together this brightly colored meal when I'm having one of those *winter is all gray, wet, and sad* kinds of days, and it always seems to do the trick.

GADO GADO SALAD

serves 4

This "salad" is made of simple-to-prepare and kid-friendly elements like rice and hard-boiled eggs. However, if your child just eats a pile of sliced mango and peanut-sauced rice, don't beat yourself up about it—every element of this meal is a whole and nutritious food.

KIDS CAN: Put kids in charge of measuring out the peanut sauce ingredients into the blender. They can also prepare the salad toppings with child-safe knives or kitchen shears.

SALAD

1½ cups brown rice, medium or short grain

8 cups water

1 tablespoon unsalted butter

1 teaspoon kosher salt

4 to 8 large eggs (however many your family wants)

4 carrots, peeled and cut into thin matchsticks or peeled into ribbons

2 mangoes, peeled, pitted, and thinly sliced

½ head purple cabbage, thinly sliced

1 cup cilantro leaves

1 cup dry roasted, lightly salted peanuts, chopped

SAUCE

¼ cup sesame seeds

¼ cup creamy peanut butter

5 tablespoons soy sauce

2 tablespoons rice vinegar

1 tablespoon honey

1 tablespoon minced fresh gingerroot

2 garlic cloves

5 tablespoons warm water

---

1. I like to boil my rice like pasta, as it always comes out perfectly and never sticks to the pan. Simply combine the rice and water in a saucepan. Bring the pot to a boil and let the rice cook away until tender, about 30 minutes. Drain, return the rice to the pot, stir in butter and salt, and cover until you are ready to assemble the salad. Fluff the rice with a fork before dishing it out.

2. While the rice cooks, cook the eggs. Put the eggs in the bottom of a medium pot and cover with water by 1 inch. Cover the pot and bring the water to a boil. As soon as the water starts to boil, turn off the heat and set a timer for 12 minutes. After 12 minutes, drain the eggs, run them under cold water, and peel. (If you like a soft yolk, set the timer for 8 minutes instead of 12.) Slice the peeled eggs and set them aside.

3. To make the sauce, simply whiz everything together in a blender.

4. You can assemble individual Gado Gado Salad bowls or make one large, family-style bowl. Either way, make a pile of rice, top it with carrots, mango, cabbage, cilantro, peanuts, and sliced eggs, then drizzle on some peanut

sauce. Extra peanut sauce can be kept in a sealed glass jar in the refrigerator for a few weeks. The sauce will become thick when chilled, so loosen it up with a splash of hot water or let it sit out on your counter to come to room temperature before using.

FOR BABY: Prepare a baby-friendly salad of brown rice, crumbled egg, and finely diced mango.

TOMORROW'S DINNER: NOODLE SALAD

Prepare extra toppings and store them in the refrigerator. Tomorrow night, cook some soba noodles and mix in the mango, shredded cabbage, carrots, and cilantro. Throw in diced chicken or drained chickpeas. Toss everything together and drizzle with soy sauce, sesame oil, lime juice, and sesame seeds.

BROILED HONEY-VANILLA GRAPEFRUITS

serves 4

It's always hard to find a fresh, bright dessert in the middle of winter. This is my best go of it—tart pink grapefruit halves covered with vanilla honey and roasted until gooey. The result is a treat that is both warming and refreshing.

KIDS CAN: Kids can mix and spread vanilla honey onto the grapefruit halves.

| 2 grapefruits, halved | 4 tablespoons honey | ½ teaspoon pure vanilla extract |

1. Set a rack about 3 inches from the broiler and set the oven to Broil. While the broiler heats, use a serrated knife to separate the grapefruit sections from the membranes. In a small bowl, mix together the honey and vanilla, then spread the mixture evenly across the cut side of each grapefruit half (the back of a small metal spoon works best). Place the fruits in a baking dish, cut sides up, and transfer them to the rack closest to the broiler. Broil until golden and bubbly, about 4 minutes.

Our Favorite Veggie Burgers

BLACK BEAN QUINOA BURGERS

ROASTED CARROTS WITH HONEY BUTTER

QUICK CITRUS-DARK CHOCOLATE CAKE

For this menu, I've paired my family's most requested veggie burgers with roasted carrots tossed in honey butter and quick chocolate cake. This is just the kind of meal I would aim for if my husband's January birthday fell on a hectic weeknight—special but totally doable with proper planning. If you don't have any winter birthdays in your family, this dessert is perfect for the holidays or as a post-snow shoveling reward to yourself.

BLACK BEAN QUINOA BURGERS

makes 4 burgers

These burgers have been the most popular meal in our house for ten years, ever since my sister served Nick and me her version when we were first dating. Now I find myself mixing up a batch every time I feel like we have nothing for dinner, quickly realizing that quinoa, black beans, and an onion are almost always in the pantry.

KIDS CAN: Little helpers can squish the burger mixture together with their hands.

½ cup dry quinoa

1 cup water

3 tablespoons olive oil, divided

½ medium yellow onion, finely chopped

2 garlic cloves, finely chopped

One 14-ounce can black beans, drained and rinsed

½ cup panko bread crumbs

1 large egg

1 teaspoon kosher salt

1 teaspoon ground cumin

1 teaspoon chili powder

1 tablespoon tomato paste

Suggested burger toppings: sliced avocado, sprouts, honey mustard, hot sauce

---

1. Combine the quinoa and water in a small saucepan. Cover the pot and bring to a boil over high heat, then reduce the heat to low and simmer until the water is absorbed, about 15 minutes.

2. Meanwhile, heat 1 tablespoon of the olive oil in a medium sauté pan. Sauté the onion and garlic until soft, about 5 minutes.

3. In a medium bowl, combine the black beans, bread crumbs, egg, salt, cumin, chili powder, and tomato paste. Add in the cooked quinoa and the sautéed onion and garlic. Using your hands, squish the mixture together until everything is well incorporated. Form 4 equal-size patties. Heat the remaining 2 tablespoons of oil in a large skillet over medium heat. Cook the burgers in the hot oil until they are brown and crisp, about 7 minutes a side. Serve with sliced avocado, sprouts, and honey mustard or hot sauce.

FOR BABY: Crumble up a quinoa burger into bits for spoon or finger feeding. Before tossing carrots in the honey butter, smash a few plain roasted carrots with the back of a fork.

TOMORROW'S DINNER: HASH AND EGGS

Prepare a second batch of quinoa burger mix and store it in the refrigerator. Tomorrow, heat a large skillet with a couple tablespoons of olive oil and spread the mix out in a single layer, cooking it into a crispy hash. Serve the quinoa-bean hash with eggs and a salad.

ROASTED CARROTS WITH HONEY BUTTER

serves 4 to 6

Some say that eating root vegetables (like carrots) makes us feel physically and mentally grounded and rooted. In the winter, I'll take all the help I can get. Here, carrot spears are roasted then tossed in a soft honey butter, making a warm, melty, sweet, and salty side dish.

KIDS CAN: Little helpers can make the honey butter.

---

10 to 12 carrots, peeled

2 to 3 tablespoons olive oil

Kosher salt and freshly ground black pepper

2 tablespoons unsalted butter, at room temperature

2 tablespoons honey

---

1. Preheat the oven to 450°F. While the oven warms, cut the peeled carrots on the diagonal into 2-inch-long slices. Toss the carrots with olive oil, a big pinch of salt, and a few grinds of pepper. Arrange the carrots in a single layer in a roasting pan, transfer them to the oven, and roast for 20 to 30 minutes, until the edges are deeply caramelized.

2. While the carrots roast, mash the butter and honey together in a large serving bowl. Toss the roasted carrots in the honey butter, taste for salt, and serve hot.

QUICK CITRUS–DARK CHOCOLATE CAKE

makes one 8-inch round cake

This cake is as dense and rich as a fudge brownie, but it's made with antioxidant-rich dark chocolate and unrefined coconut sugar for a healthier take on a flourless chocolate dessert. A thin slice goes a long way. I like to top the cake with fresh whipped cream and thin blood orange slices for a citrus kick.

---

7 ounces dark chocolate (60 to 70% cacao)

14 tablespoons unsalted butter, cut into 1-inch cubes

1⅓ cups coconut sugar

5 large eggs

1 tablespoon unbleached all-purpose flour

3 tablespoons freshly squeezed orange juice

Whipped cream and thinly sliced blood orange, for serving

---

1. Preheat the oven to 375˚F and butter an 8-inch round cake pan. Line the base of the cake pan with parchment paper.

2. Finely chop the chocolate with a serrated knife. Place the chopped chocolate in a small saucepan with the butter and gently melt the mixture over low heat, stirring regularly. Add the coconut sugar to the melted chocolate-butter mixture, stir well, and set the saucepan aside to cool for a few moments.

3. Add the eggs one by one to the chocolate mixture, whisking well after each addition. Add the flour and orange juice and stir to combine. Pour the batter into the prepared cake pan and bake for approximately 20 to 25 minutes, or until the center of the cake looks just set and the top looks shiny and a bit crackly.

4. Remove the cake from the oven and let it cool in the pan on a wire rack for 10 minutes, then carefully invert the cake onto the wire rack and peel off the parchment paper. Allow the cake to cool completely (or the whipped cream will melt right off). The cake will deflate slightly as it cools. Serve the rich cake topped with whipped cream and blood orange slices.

The Moriartys' Family Meal, St. Johnsbury, Vermont

CHICKEN TORTILLA SOUP

CHURROS WITH MEXICAN CHOCOLATE DIPPING SAUCE

shared by Ashleigh Moriarty

When I was growing up, my English mom made a complete roast dinner every Sunday, which always made our house feel comforting and cozy. Now that I have my own family, I try to carry on this tradition as often as possible. Our very long, cold Vermont winters make it a necessity to cook meals that fill the family and house with warmth. This Chicken Tortilla Soup is a perfect snowy day recipe, but don't be afraid to make it in other seasons, as the flavors complement the warm spring and summer months as well. In fact, the first time we had Chicken Tortilla Soup was on a sweltering beach in Mexico. Perhaps we make this often in the cold winter to try to channel that beachy feeling again.

CHICKEN TORTILLA SOUP

serves 4 to 6

Whenever I roast a whole chicken, I use the leftovers to make a rich broth for the base of this soup. I put the picked-over chicken carcass in the slow cooker and let it cook for 8 to 12 hours to make an easy, hands-off stock. Our daughters help prepare all the yummy soup garnishes, such as the tortillas, grated cheese, and cilantro. They especially enjoy this interactive dinner, as they are able to pick and pile on whatever toppings they like.

KIDS CAN: Kids can prepare the tortilla strips by slicing the corn tortillas with a pizza cutter, tossing them in oil, and arranging them on a baking sheet.

---

1 medium yellow onion

2 garlic cloves

½ to 1 jalapeño pepper, seeds and membranes removed

3 tablespoons olive oil, divided

One 14-ounce can diced tomatoes

1 teaspoon plus a pinch of kosher salt, divided

6 cups Slow Cooker Chicken Stock (recipe follows) or low-sodium chicken broth

4 cups shredded chicken (from a 4- to 5-pound roasted chicken)

Juice of 1 lime

8 small corn tortillas

SLOW COOKER CHICKEN STOCK

One 4- to 5-pound chicken, roasted, meat removed

2 celery ribs

2 carrots

2 medium onions, halved

2 bay leaves

Small handful herbs of your choice (such as parsley or thyme), optional

TOPPINGS

Sour cream

Lime wedges

Chopped cilantro

Sliced avocado

Hot sauce

---

1. To make the stock, place the chicken carcass, celery, carrots, onions, and bay leaves in a 6-quart slow cooker. Add any herbs. Cover with water and cook on low for at least 8 and up to 24 hours. Using a fine-mesh sieve, strain the finished stock into a large pot.

2. When you're ready to make the soup, preheat the oven to 375°F. In a food processor, whiz the onion, garlic, and jalapeño into a fine paste.

3. Heat 2 tablespoons of the oil in a large soup pot over medium heat and sauté the onion mixture until soft, 5 to 7 minutes. Add the tomatoes, 1 teaspoon of the salt, the broth, shredded chicken, and lime juice. Bring the soup to a boil, reduce the heat to low, and simmer for 5 minutes or until everything is heated through.

4. Slice the corn tortillas into ¼-inch-thick strips

(continued)

(this is easy with a pizza cutter). In a large bowl, toss the tortilla strips with the remaining 1 tablespoon of oil and the remaining pinch of salt, then arrange them in a single layer on a rimmed baking sheet. Toast the tortilla strips in the oven until crisp, about 10 minutes. To serve, place some tortilla strips in the bottom of each bowl, ladle the soup over the top, and pile on the toppings.

FOR BABY: Depending on your baby's age and tastes, omit or reduce the amount of jalapeño in the soup. Pulse a bowl of soup and a few avocado slices in the food processor, or whiz the mixture with an immersion blender to create a creamy consistency. Older infants can enjoy the soup as is.

CHURROS WITH MEXICAN CHOCOLATE DIPPING SAUCE

makes 18 churros

This dessert is popular in our house because the girls can, to their delight, make the churros themselves with minimal supervision.

KIDS CAN: Little helpers can prepare the churros by sprinkling on the cinnamon-sugar mixture, then cutting and twisting the dough.

CHURROS

½ cup pure cane sugar

2 tablespoons ground cinnamon

1 sheet frozen puff pastry dough, defrosted

MEXICAN CHOCOLATE DIPPING SAUCE

½ cup heavy cream

¾ cup chopped Mexican chocolate (Taza Cacao Puro is our favorite)

Pinch of ground cinnamon

Up to ½ teaspoon cayenne or ancho chili powder (optional, depending on your family's heat tolerance)

---

1. To make the churros, preheat the oven to 375°F. Mix the sugar and cinnamon together in a small bowl. Sprinkle half of the mixture over a sheet of parchment paper and lay the defrosted puff pastry on top. Cut the puff pastry into 1-inch-thick strips (the short way) and brush them with water. Sprinkle the wet strips with the remaining cinnamon-sugar mixture. Hold both ends of each strip and twist it 2 to 3 times before placing it on a baking sheet. Repeat with the remaining strips. Bake for 20 minutes or until puffy and golden.

2. While the churros are baking, combine the cream and chocolate in a small saucepan and warm the mixture over low heat, whisking constantly until the chocolate begins to melt, about 3 minutes. Stir in the cinnamon and chili powder (if using). Continue whisking until the chocolate is melted and the ingredients are combined, about 5 minutes. Serve the churros with individual pots of warm dipping sauce.

Kids Eating Fish

COD CAKES WITH POACHED EGGS

QUICK ARUGULA SALAD

SLOW COOKER BROWN RICE PUDDING

Once Columbus Day comes and goes, many shops, restaurants, and homes around us lock up for the next seven months. Thankfully, a handful of our favorite spots stay open to support us through this most trying stretch. There is a diner in town that we frequent on cold, early mornings—we run into friends, drink too much coffee, and say yes to the boys' requests of chocolate chip pancakes. My menu favorite is a codfish cake served with poached eggs and greens. This winter meal is inspired by that favorite diner breakfast. The cakes' crispy, golden edges and potato filling help to convince all family members that a crispy fish cake is worth trying.

COD CAKES WITH POACHED EGGS

serves 4

Our kids love New England clam chowder, but it's a challenge to hook them on other seafood dinners (you ironic island kids, you). These cakes are my best attempt at getting some fish into our boys—sometimes it succeeds, and other times one of them ends up eating a couple of eggs for dinner. Such is life. I like my cod cake with a runny poached egg, but sunny-side up or scrambled eggs are just as good. A quick arugula salad pairs well with this rich dish. I just toss baby arugula with olive oil, lemon juice, salt, and pepper.

---

1 tablespoon fresh thyme leaves

3 tablespoons minced fresh chives

2 tablespoons Dijon mustard

1 tablespoon real mayonnaise

1 teaspoon kosher salt

½ teaspoon freshly grated orange zest

1 to 2 large Yukon gold potatoes, peeled and cut into 1-inch cubes (about 2 cups)

1 pound filleted codfish

¾ cup panko bread crumbs

¼ cup extra virgin olive oil

Splash of white vinegar

4 large eggs

Lemon wedges, for serving

---

1. In a medium bowl, combine the thyme, chives, mustard, mayonnaise, salt, and orange zest. Stir everything to combine.

2. Place the cubed potatoes in a large, high-sided skillet and cover with water. Bring the water to a boil over high heat, reduce the heat to low, cover, and simmer the potatoes until tender, about 7 minutes. Using a slotted spoon, remove the cooked potatoes from the skillet and place them in a small bowl. Do not drain the skillet. Mash the potatoes with a fork and set them aside.

3. Return the skillet to the stove over high heat, bring the potato cooking water to a boil, and then carefully slide in the cod fillets. Turn the heat down to the lowest setting, cover, and poach the fish until just flaky and cooked through, about 5 minutes. Remove from the water and gently flake the fish apart, then fold it into the mashed potatoes. Add the potato-cod mixture to the mustard mixture and add in the bread crumbs. Carefully fold everything to combine (you want to keep big flakes of fish).

4. Heat the olive oil in a large cast iron skillet set over medium heat. While it heats, use your hands to divide the cod cake mixture into four large patties. Cook the cakes in the hot oil for 5 to 7 minutes per side or until crisp and golden.

5. While the cakes fry up, poach your eggs. Fill a pot with a few inches of water and add the vinegar. Put the pot over medium-high heat and

warm it until the water is just starting to bubble or simmer. This is the temperature you want to stick with. Crack the first egg into a small bowl or ramekin. Gently slide the egg into the hot water and let it cook for 3 to 4 minutes. Remove the egg with a slotted spoon and place it directly onto a kitchen towel to absorb any excess water. Repeat this process with the rest of the eggs. You can cook more than one egg at a time if your pot is large enough.

6. Place a poached egg on the top of each cod cake and serve immediately with lemon wedges and a quick arugula salad (see the note in the recipe's introduction).

FOR BABY: The soft texture of cod cakes is perfect for baby. Either mix a runny poached egg into baby's cod cake or prepare an egg in their favorite style to serve on the side.

TOMORROW'S DINNER: GREEN HOME FRIES

Boil a second pot of potatoes. Tomorrow, place a large cast iron skillet over medium-high heat. Add some butter, sliced cooked potatoes, and 4 cups of baby spinach. Cook until the potatoes are crisp and the spinach is wilted, 7 to 10 minutes. Eat with local sausages, bacon, and/or eggs.

SLOW COOKER BROWN RICE PUDDING

serves 4 to 6

This rice pudding is one of my favorite winter treats, as you simply mix the ingredients together in the slow cooker, turn it on, and later that day enjoy a warm, nutritious pudding without lifting a finger. Bonus—your house smells like a bakery.

KIDS CAN: In the morning, little ones can measure the rice pudding ingredients into the slow cooker, and after dinner kids can whip the cream, crush the pecans, and shave the dark chocolate with a vegetable peeler.

¾ cup long-grain brown rice

4½ cups whole milk, divided

¾ cup coconut sugar (or any granulated sweetener)

1 teaspoon ground cinnamon

1 teaspoon pure vanilla extract

Pinch of kosher salt

5 tablespoons unsalted butter, melted

FOR SERVING (OPTIONAL)

Whipped cream

Chopped pecans

Shaved dark chocolate

---

1. In a 6-quart slow cooker, mix together the rice, 3½ cups of the milk, the sugar, cinnamon, vanilla, salt, and melted butter. Cover the slow cooker and cook on high for 4 to 4½ hours, until the rice is tender (taste the rice around 4 hours). Just before serving, stir in the remaining cup of milk. Top the pudding with whipped cream, chopped pecans, and dark chocolate shavings.

FOR BABY: Brown rice pudding is a soft, sweet treat babies can enjoy.

Orange and Green Pasta Bowls

CREAMY PUMPKIN FETTUCCINE

PUMPKIN SEED PESTO

ROASTED BROCCOLINI

Winter food cravings are serious things, not to be ignored. You can't help but dream of cheesy casseroles, warming soups, and rich chocolate after shoveling feet of snow, turning on the lights at 4 P.M., and slathering moisturizer on dry, patchy skin, day after day. We need incentives to keep up with life's pace in unapologetic weather (and I'm not just talking wine here). This dinner has all those things we look for in winter comfort food, but also offers healthy doses of spinach, nutrient-dense pumpkin seeds, and Broccolini. I like to eat the Creamy Pumpkin Fettuccine, Pumpkin Seed Pesto, and Roasted Broccolini piled high together in one bowl. Extra pesto is delicious in omelets, as a sandwich spread, or tossed with roasted root vegetables.

CREAMY PUMPKIN FETTUCCINE

serves 4 to 6

This pasta dinner offers two delicious sauces—creamy pumpkin and Pumpkin Seed Pesto (recipe follows). Ideally, you would eat the fettuccine tossed in the creamy pumpkin sauce with a dollop of pesto on top. That said, if you have time for only one sauce, or if your family naturally gravitates to one type over the other, the fettuccine is delicious served with either one. To make the most of your time, prepare the pesto and get the Broccolini in the oven right when you put the pot of pasta water on to boil.

KIDS CAN: Little helpers can whisk together the cream sauce ingredients.

½ pound dried fettuccine

½ pound dried spinach fettuccine

5 ounces grated Parmesan cheese, plus more for serving

3 tablespoons heavy cream

1 large egg

⅔ cup pureed cooked or canned pumpkin (or any winter squash)

1 teaspoon arrowroot powder or cornstarch

3 tablespoons extra virgin olive oil, plus more for serving

½ teaspoon freshly grated lemon zest

Kosher salt and freshly ground black pepper

Pumpkin Seed Pesto (recipe follows)

---

1. Bring a big pot of salted water to a boil over high heat. When the water comes to a rolling boil, cook the pastas together per the package instructions, shaving 1 minute off the suggested cooking time. Just before draining the pasta, scoop 1 cup of hot pasta water from the pot and reserve it for the sauce. Drain the pasta and set it aside.

2. While the pasta cooks, whisk together the Parmesan cheese, cream, egg, pureed pumpkin, arrowroot powder, olive oil, and lemon zest in a medium bowl. Whisk in the reserved pasta water. Season the sauce with salt and pepper.

3. Return your pasta pot to medium-high heat and pour in the sauce. Bring the pumpkin sauce to a boil, then turn down the heat to a simmer. Cook the sauce for 2 to 3 minutes, just until it has thickened, then add the pasta to the pot. Toss the pasta and sauce together and serve it with dollops of Pumpkin Seed Pesto and the Roasted Broccolini (recipes follow).

PUMPKIN SEED PESTO

makes about 1½ cups

The best thing about pesto is that it is, almost always, green. Because of this, when a new bowl of vibrant pesto sauce hits our dinner table, the boys don't question the ingredients as long as they see that familiar green color. We have experimented with a wide variety of pestos at our house, from kale to artichoke and sun-dried tomato. This rich and nutty Pumpkin Seed Pesto is my favorite thing for adding a salty bite to creamy pastas and soups.

---

1 cup toasted pumpkin seeds	Zest and juice of 1 lemon	½ teaspoon kosher salt
1½ cups baby spinach	1 garlic clove	¼ cup extra virgin olive oil

---

1. Simply whiz everything together in a food processor. Extra pesto can be stored in an airtight glass jar in the refrigerator for up to 1 week.

TOMORROW'S DINNER: PANINI

Slice a loaf of hearty, whole-wheat bread. Spread the slices with leftover pesto, then layer on Monterey Jack cheese, sliced turkey breast, and sliced tomatoes. Grill in a lightly buttered cast iron skillet, weighting the sandwiches down with a heavy pot.

ROASTED BROCCOLINI

serves 4

Broccolini is similar to broccoli but with smaller florets and long, thin stalks. Many cultures stir-fry the vegetable (which is delicious), but I like to roast it in the oven, as the stalks hold up well under high heat. Nutritionally, it is high in vitamin C and contains vitamin A, calcium, folate, and iron.

KIDS CAN: Children can toss the Broccolini with the oil and salt.

1 bunch Broccolini, trimmed	1 tablespoon olive oil	Big pinch kosher salt

1. Preheat the oven to 400°F. Toss the Broccolini with the olive oil and salt. Arrange the Broccolini in an even layer on a baking sheet. Roast until crisp and tender, about 20 minutes.

FOR BABY: Make a small bowl of pumpkin pasta, Broccolini, and pesto for baby. Finely chop or whiz the dinner in a food processor to create the ideal texture. For older infants, chopped Broccolini is an easy finger food.

Winter Sunday Supper
(and a Campfire Party)

KALE AND SWEET POTATO TACOS

CORN TORTILLAS

SLOW COOKER BLACK BEANS

HONEY MARSHMALLOWS

Before we moved to Martha's Vineyard, we lived in Providence, Rhode Island. I worked downtown, right around the corner from a great little taco shop. Nick's grad-school building was a short walk away, so every Friday we would meet and treat ourselves to a taco lunch. I always ordered the special veggie taco of the day— piled high with kale ribbons, roasted sweet potatoes, or charred mushrooms. This dinner reminds me of that time of our lives, however far off it feels today.

KALE AND SWEET POTATO TACOS

serves 6

For these tacos, we layer warm vegetables, slightly sweet black beans (made in the slow cooker!), and avocado cream onto homemade corn tortillas. If you have a lazy Sunday, it's fun to make all the components yourself, but without the time it's fine to use store-bought tortillas and canned beans instead.

TACO FILLINGS

3 sweet potatoes

1 large bunch kale

3 tablespoons olive oil, divided

Kosher salt

⅓ cup water

AVOCADO CREAM

2 avocados

2 tablespoons sour cream or plain full-fat yogurt

Juice from ½ lime

2 big pinches kosher salt

Slow Cooker Black Beans (page 82)

Corn Tortillas (page 80)

1 cup chopped fresh cilantro, for serving

Hot sauce, for serving

Lime wedges, for serving

---

1. Prepare the vegetables. Peel the potatoes and dice them into ⅛-inch cubes (they need to be small to cook through in the skillet). Prepare the kale by removing the stems and slicing the leaves into thin ribbons. Heat 2 tablespoons of the oil in a large cast iron skillet over medium heat. Add the potatoes, sprinkle with salt, and spread them out in a single layer. Cover the skillet (use a baking sheet if you don't have a large lid), and cook for 10 minutes (tossing once), until fork-tender. Add in the kale ribbons, another sprinkle of salt, and the water. Toss to combine, cover again, and cook for another 10 minutes, until the kale is wilted (tossing once). Taste and add more salt if needed.

2. While the vegetables are cooking, make the avocado cream. Do this by mashing the avocados, sour cream, lime juice, and salt together in a small bowl.

3. To serve, pile black beans and vegetables into fresh corn tortillas. Top with avocado cream, chopped cilantro, hot sauce, and a squirt of fresh lime juice.

FOR BABY: In a small bowl, mash together some sweet potato, kale, and beans. Spoon-feed the mixture while baby holds and munches on a soft tortilla.

TOMORROW'S DINNER: VEGETABLE FRITTATA

Prepare a second skillet of sweet potatoes and kale. Tomorrow, mix the vegetables with 7 whisked eggs, ⅓ cup of milk, ⅓ cup of cream, salt, pepper, and a dash of Worcestershire sauce. Transfer the mixture to an oven-safe skillet and bake at 375°F until set, about 25 minutes.

CORN TORTILLAS

makes about 12 tortillas

If you don't already own a tortilla press, it is one of the one-trick kitchen gadgets I recommend. They are inexpensive, easy to use, and make the most delicious homemade corn tortillas. Kids will especially love rolling out and pressing the soft tortilla dough.

2 cups masa harina (we like Bob's Red Mill Masa Harina Golden Corn Flour)	½ teaspoon kosher salt	1½ to 2 cups water

1. In a large mixing bowl, stir together the masa harina and salt. Add 1¼ to 1½ cups of the water, a little at a time, stirring between each addition until the dough just comes together into a ball. Cover the bowl with plastic wrap and let it sit at room temperature for 15 to 30 minutes. At this point the dough will be too dry and crumbly to work with. Add the remaining ½ to ¾ cup of water, a little at a time, and mix until you can make smooth balls of the dough without its sticking to your hands. Cover the bowl and set it aside.

2. Preheat two large skillets, one over medium-high heat and one over high heat.

3. Line a shallow bowl with a large, clean kitchen towel. Cut a plastic bag into two rounds about the size of the tortilla press. Place a 1-inch ball of dough in the center of the first piece of plastic. Press down on the dough to flatten it some. If the dough cracks at this point, it's a little too dry: return the dough to the ball, mix in a little more water, and start again. Add the second piece of plastic on top of the flattened dough, then transfer the dough and plastic to the tortilla press and press the tortilla firmly. Open it, rotate the tortilla 90 degrees, and press it again. Peel off the top piece of plastic. Carefully peel the tortilla off the bottom piece of plastic and place it in the skillet set over medium-high heat. Once it sets and can be slid around (after about 1 minute), flip the tortilla and transfer it to the skillet set over high heat. When the tortilla puffs slightly, flip it again (keeping it over high heat) and cook for another 30 seconds until it gets a nice color and puffs a little more. Transfer the tortilla to the kitchen towel–lined bowl and fold the towel over it. Repeat this process with the remaining tortilla dough, keeping the warm tortillas under wraps of the towel. It goes pretty fast once you get into a rhythm. Extra corn tortillas can be wrapped tightly and stored on the counter for up to 2 days. To reheat, dampen the tortillas with wet hands and warm them in a skillet.

SLOW COOKER BLACK BEANS

makes 6 cups

I was always intimidated by cooking dried beans. I would either forget to soak them ahead of time (AHHHH!) or keep them simmering in a pot, only to find them undercooked at the end of the day. After a while, I began to shy away from recipes that suggested I try it again. Discovering the simplicity of preparing dried beans in the slow cooker has thrown my trepidation out the window. You just combine a few ingredients and turn on the machine—a few hours later you have a perfect pot of beans. Life changing.

2 cups dried black beans, picked over and rinsed

4 cups water

1 teaspoon ground cumin

½ teaspoon kosher salt (plus more to finish)

3 garlic cloves

½ medium yellow onion

¼ navel orange

1. Combine everything in a 6-quart slow cooker, cover, and cook on high for 4 hours. After 4 hours, turn the slow cooker to the "keep warm" setting until you're ready to eat. Taste and add more salt if needed.

HONEY MARSHMALLOWS

makes 60 to 100 marshmallows, depending on size

The winter months are isolating, so I try to find any excuse to lure friends over to our house. These Honey Marshmallows are a treat we make on lazy weekends to roast outside over a simple campfire with friends. The process of making homemade marshmallows is as much a fun science experiment as a dessert. It naturally pulls the kids into the kitchen. Marshmallows are typically full of refined sugar, but these beauties are mostly water and honey.

KIDS CAN: Kids will love helping with all the marshmallow steps, including watching the mix turn into marshmallow cream and dusting the squares with powdered sugar.

---

1 tablespoon canola oil, plus more for cutting the marshmallow

3 tablespoons gelatin

1 cup water, divided

1 cup honey

1½ teaspoons pure vanilla extract (see Note)

1 cup confectioners' sugar, for dusting

NOTE: You can replace vanilla with another extract, such as peppermint, orange, or almond, using more or less depending on the potency of the extract.

1. Grease a 13 by 9-inch baking dish with 1 tablespoon of oil and line it with parchment paper.

2. In the bowl of a stand mixer, whisk together the gelatin and ½ cup of the water. Let sit until the gelatin softens up, about 5 minutes.

3. In a small saucepan, combine the remaining ½ cup of water with the honey and vanilla. Clip a candy thermometer to the inside of the pan and bring the mixture to a boil over medium-high heat until it reaches 240°F (the soft ball stage), about 10 minutes. As soon as it reaches 240°F, turn the mixer on low and pour the hot honey mixture into the gelatin while beating. Increase the mixer speed to high and beat until fluffy

marshmallow cream forms, about 10 minutes. Pour the whipped marshmallow into the prepared baking dish and smooth the top. Leave the pan on the counter to set for at least 4 or up to 24 hours.

4. When you are ready to cut the marshmallow, dust your countertop with the confectioners' sugar. Invert the marshmallow out of the pan onto the sugar. Peel away the parchment paper. Grease a knife with canola oil and slice the marshmallow into 1 to 2-inch squares. Toss the cut marshmallows in a pile of confectioners' sugar. Extra marshmallows can be stored at room temperature in an airtight, parchment paper–lined tin for up to two weeks.

Spring

Spring is the universal light at the end of the tunnel. It is the prize for once again surviving a cold, dark winter, and in our case, one on an island with two very energetic young boys. I spend most of February daydreaming about stepping off the front porch into a sixty-degree day, and when it finally happens—man oh man— nothing is better. I have an idealistic view of spring on which I place many of my hopes: "Oh, he'll sleep until 7 A.M. in the spring" and "I will never feel overwhelmed in May!" are some of my optimistic thoughts. The funny thing is, most of the time the season lives up to my expectations (well, not the 7 A.M. part), and even when it doesn't, the strawberries, asparagus, and hours in the dirt overwhelm me with gratitude and make me forget my worries. Spring dinners are lighter (Oven-Baked Falafel with Garden Radishes, Cucumber, and Pea Shoots, page 90) and more colorful (Leek, Red Potato, and Feta Galette, page 96), and they show off what is sprouting outside (Rhubarb Sundaes, page 100). They also offer a variety of raw, colorful foods packed with antioxidants to help detox weary winter bodies and clean out their dusty systems. When the time is right, grab a blanket and eat outside, even if it's in your driveway. We waited too long for this season to stay indoors.

Spring Meals

89
A SPRING PICNIC
Oven-Baked Falafel with Garden Radishes, Cucumber, and Pea Shoots

Roasted Asparagus

95
FROZEN PASTRY CRUST TO RESCUE
Leek, Red Potato, and Feta Galette

Spring Salad with Buttermilk-Herb Dressing

Rhubarb Sundaes

103
MORE PEAS, PLEASE!
Sweet Pea Oven Risotto

Garlicky Pea Shoots

Strawberries with Vanilla Sugar

109
THE SOLONS' FAMILY MEAL
Herby Pasta with Mussels and Leeks

Caesar-ish Salad with Rosemary Croutons

Rhubarb Cake with Vanilla Crème Fraîche

115
A SAVORY (AND VERY GREEN) PIE
Skillet Spinach Pie

Puffed Brown Rice Treats

119
FOR THE BUSIEST NIGHT
Slow Cooker Indian Butter Chicken with Sweet Peas

Lemon-Pecan Shortbread Cookies

125
RAINY SPRING DAYS NEED STEW (AND BREAD)
Chickpea Stew with Broccoli Pesto

Simple Dutch Oven Bread

131
MAGIC WORD—"NOODLES!"
Sesame Noodles with Bok Choy and Sweet Peppers

Cilantro-Lime Grilled Tuna

137
A PLATE OF SPRING COLORS
Red Lentils with Coconut Milk and Spinach

Black Rice with Dried Peaches and Almonds

Chocolate-Mint Milkshakes

143
SPRING SUNDAY SUPPER
Splayed Roast Chicken with Spring Vegetables

Lemon–Red Bulgur Salad

Smashed Potatoes

Strawberry-Orange Slab Pie

A Spring Picnic

OVEN-BAKED FALAFEL WITH GARDEN RADISHES, CUCUMBER, AND PEA SHOOTS

ROASTED ASPARAGUS

This is a perfect dinner for nights when your cupboards are bare (I seem to always have these ingredients hiding someplace) and your energy is low (just whiz everything in the food processor and bake). Depending on your family's likes, you can serve the falafel balls packed in pita pockets with yogurt sauce and fresh vegetables, on top of a large green salad, or on a platter next to other nibbles, such as olives, cucumbers, tomatoes, and tzatziki and hummus dips. In my opinion, there is no wrong way to eat a warm, homemade falafel ball (especially if you are doing so outside on the green grass).

OVEN-BAKED FALAFEL WITH GARDEN RADISHES, CUCUMBER, AND PEA SHOOTS

makes 15 small balls

My sister Anna made us a version of these falafel rounds almost ten years ago. I immediately quizzed her on the recipe and have been serving it ever since. Our favorite method is to fill toasted pita pockets with falafel balls, then stuff in favorite crunchy vegetables, such as carrots, sprouts, radishes, cucumbers, or pea shoots. Here, I have included a simple yogurt sauce, but spreading the pitas with hummus works fine, too.

KIDS CAN: Little helpers can measure and blend the falafel ingredients and scoop and flatten the falafel balls.

FALAFEL

½ medium yellow onion

One 15-ounce can chickpeas, drained and rinsed

Handful of fresh parsley

Juice of ½ lemon

1 teaspoon ground cumin

1 teaspoon kosher salt

¼ teaspoon red pepper flakes (optional)

3 garlic cloves

4 tablespoons whole-wheat all-purpose flour (or gluten-free all-purpose flour)

2 tablespoons olive oil, divided

YOGURT SAUCE

1 cup plain full-fat Greek yogurt

3-inch piece cucumber, grated

Juice of ½ lemon

1 tablespoon chopped fresh dill

Kosher salt and freshly ground black pepper

FOR SERVING

4 pita pockets or lavash, warmed in the oven

Thinly sliced cucumber

Thinly sliced radishes

Thinly sliced red onion

Roughly chopped pea shoots

---

1. Preheat the oven to 400°F. To make the falafel, simply whiz all the ingredients (leaving out 1 tablespoon of the olive oil) in a food processor until mostly smooth (with a few remaining chunks).

2. Grease a baking sheet with the remaining tablespoon of olive oil. Using a tablespoon measure, place heaping scoops of the falafel mixture on the baking sheet, then flatten them with the back of the spoon. Bake the falafel rounds for 10 minutes, flip them, and then bake for another 10 minutes, until edges are crisp and tops are golden.

3. While the falafel bakes, mix together all the sauce ingredients in a medium bowl.

4. Serve the baked falafel with warm pita pockets or lavash, yogurt sauce, sliced vegetables, and pea shoots.

FOR BABY: For older babies, smash a falafel ball inside a small wedge of pita bread and top with yogurt sauce. Younger babies will enjoy small pieces of falafel and thin slices of peeled cucumber.

TOMORROW'S DINNER: CHICKEN KABOBS

Grill chicken kabobs and top the skewers with extra yogurt sauce and chopped vegetables.

ROASTED ASPARAGUS

serves 4

Roasted asparagus often finds its way onto our table in the spring because stalk snapping is Dylan's favorite kitchen job. When asparagus is around, I am guaranteed a few quiet minutes to throw dinner together while he works on the floor.

KIDS CAN: Everyone can snap asparagus stalks, of course!

---

1 bunch asparagus, ends trimmed	2 tablespoons extra virgin olive oil	Big pinch of kosher salt

---

1. Preheat the oven to 400°F. In a large bowl, toss the trimmed asparagus with the oil and salt. Arrange the spears in a single layer on a rimmed baking sheet. Roast the asparagus for 20 to 25 minutes, until tips are crisp. (You can roast them ahead, or stick them in the oven with the falafel.)

FOR BABY: Asparagus can be stringy, so chop it well before offering it as a finger food.

Frozen Pastry Crust to the Rescue

LEEK, RED POTATO, AND FETA GALETTE

SPRING SALAD WITH BUTTERMILK-HERB DRESSING

RHUBARB SUNDAES

This dinner is all about the art of frozen pastry. I highly recommend making a batch of pastry when you score fifteen extra minutes and freezing it for impromptu galettes and quiches. That way, all you have to do is toss the frozen dough in the refrigerator in the morning to defrost and, come dinnertime, fill it with any combination of vegetables, cheese, and eggs you like. For especially desperate afternoons, kids can stamp cookies from a rolled-out round of pastry dough. Simply sprinkle the stamped shapes with cinnamon and coconut sugar, then bake at 350°F until golden—that is sure to lighten the mood.

LEEK, RED POTATO, AND FETA GALETTE

serves 4 to 6

A galette is simply a flat, round, freeform pastry thing. You can fill it with whatever you'd like, and it is not supposed to look neat. Here, I combine thinly sliced red potatoes, leeks, dill, feta, and lemon for a fresh bake. I encourage you to adapt this combination to your own tastes—perhaps trying crumbled goat cheese in place of the feta or tossing in a handful of leftover crumbled bacon. Keep in mind that you will need to thaw the frozen dough in the refrigerator overnight and then allow it to warm up on the counter for 15 minutes before rolling it out.

KIDS CAN: Set up a big pot of water for kids to wash and clean the sliced leeks.

CRUST

2 cups unbleached all-purpose flour, plus more for dusting

½ teaspoon kosher salt

1 cup (2 sticks) cold unsalted butter, cut into ½-inch cubes

¼ cup ice water

FILLING

2 tablespoons extra virgin olive oil

3 leeks, white and light green parts thinly sliced (about 2½ cups)

3 medium red potatoes, sliced into ⅛-inch-thick rounds

½ teaspoon kosher salt

5 grinds of black pepper

2 tablespoons chopped fresh dill

4 tablespoons crumbled feta cheese

Juice of ½ lemon

1. To make the crust, measure the flour and salt into a food processor, then pulse a few times to combine. Add the butter cubes and continue to pulse until the butter bits are the size of peas. Next, turn the motor on and stream in the ice water, starting with ¼ cup, then adding a bit more if the dough looks really sandy. Continue to run the motor until the dough just begins to form a ball. Turn the motor off.

2. Dust a work surface with flour, then turn out the dough and gently form it into a ball. Flatten the ball into a disk. Wrap the dough in plastic and store it in the refrigerator for at least 10 minutes and up to 24 hours. (Or place the wrapped dough in the freezer to use at a future date.)

3. To make the galette, preheat the oven to 375°F.

4. Clean the sliced leeks in a large bowl of water—gritty soil often hides between the vegetable's layers. Dry the washed leeks well on a kitchen towel.

5. In a large sauté pan, warm the olive oil over medium heat. Add the dry leeks, sliced potatoes,

(continued)

salt, and pepper. Cook until the vegetables are soft, gently tossing, about 10 minutes. Turn off the heat and add in the chopped dill, crumbled feta, and lemon juice. Allow the filling to cool slightly as you roll out the pastry dough.

6. Dust the counter with flour and roll the dough disk into a 14-inch-thick round. Don't worry about creating a perfect circle! Fill the middle of the pastry with the vegetable mixture, leaving a 1-inch border of dough all the way around. Fold the border of dough up around the filling and bake for 25 to 30 minutes, until the crust is slightly golden.

FOR BABY: Older babies can happily nibble on bite-size pieces of galette. For infants needing softer foods, puree portions of the leeks and potatoes.

TOMORROW'S DINNER: VEGETABLE FRITTATA
Prepare a second batch of leeks and red potatoes in an oven-safe skillet. Mix the vegetables with 7 whisked eggs, ⅓ cup of milk, ⅓ cup of cream, salt, pepper, and a dash of Worcestershire sauce. Bake at 375°F until set, about 25 minutes.

SPRING SALAD WITH BUTTERMILK-HERB DRESSING

serves 4; makes about 1 cup

A simple salad of baby spring lettuce makes a perfect complement to the galette. Buttermilk-Herb Dressing is a special way to dress the greens. I often fill a small bowl with olives and serve them alongside the creamy salad for a little briny bite.

KIDS CAN: This dressing is a perfect project for little helpers—throw all the ingredients into a glass jar, tighten the lid, and shake, shake, shake.

DRESSING

½ cup plain full-fat Greek yogurt

½ cup buttermilk

1 tablespoon chopped fresh basil

1 tablespoon chopped fresh chives

1 tablespoon chopped fresh dill

2 teaspoons apple cider vinegar

1 teaspoon pure cane sugar

1 teaspoon Worcestershire sauce

Big pinch of kosher salt

A few grinds of black pepper

4 cups baby lettuce leaves

---

1. Combine all the dressing ingredients in a large jar. Screw on a tight-fitting lid and shake vigorously to combine. Gently toss the baby lettuce with 4 tablespoons dressing (add more to taste) and serve immediately. Buttermilk-Herb Dressing can be stored in the refrigerator for 1 week.

RHUBARB SUNDAES

makes about 6 sundaes

For a special end to this meal, try a quick rhubarb topping for vanilla ice cream. The fruit sauce is straightforward and creates a simple sundae reminiscent of warm pie à la mode.

KIDS CAN: At dessert time, children can mix the chutney ingredients and pick mint leaves to top the sundaes.

---

3 rhubarb stalks, finely chopped (about 2 cups)

Pinch of kosher salt

½ teaspoon pure vanilla extract

1 cinnamon stick

2 tablespoons honey

Juice of ½ lemon

Vanilla ice cream, for serving

Mint leaves, for serving (optional)

Sugar cones, for serving (optional)

---

1. Preheat the oven to 325°F. Combine the chopped rhubarb, salt, vanilla, cinnamon stick, honey, and lemon juice in a baking dish or small ovenproof saucepan. Toss the ingredients to combine and cover the dish or pan with a lid. Bake for 30 minutes, until slightly thickened and fragrant. Remove the chutney from the oven and set it aside to cool.

2. Top scoops of vanilla ice cream with warm or room-temperature rhubarb chutney, and, if desired, add a few fresh mint leaves and a little cone hat to each serving. Refrigerate extra chutney in an airtight glass jar and enjoy within 1 week.

More Peas, Please!

SWEET PEA OVEN RISOTTO

GARLICKY PEA SHOOTS

STRAWBERRIES WITH VANILLA SUGAR

There were a few years there when the boys would eat only *frozen* peas. I found this to be so odd until I wrote about it and discovered that it is a common thread among toddlers and preschoolers—who knew? Happily, that frozen pea stage upped their pea confidence, so now they are more likely to welcome the little sweet vegetable in other (warmer . . . cooked) forms. Most recently, Dylan showed me the pea shoots growing in his preschool garden and quickly requested them at dinnertime. The thin, delicate shoots are sweet, tender, and a delicious addition to any spring meal. Lucky for me, Dylan discovered this vegetable on his own, and this ownership makes him happy to see, talk about, and eat the green shoots again and again.

SWEET PEA OVEN RISOTTO

serves 6

The first time I visited Nick's childhood home in New York, my now mother-in-law, Polly, made a version of this risotto for dinner. I was so impressed by the texture of the rice that I immediately asked for the recipe. Since then, this versatile, comforting risotto has been our favorite meal to please a crowd. Here, I toss in some sweet peas, but roasted cherry tomatoes, caramelized winter squash, and sautéed mushrooms are delicious, too.

---

4 tablespoons extra virgin olive oil

4 shallots, finely chopped

2 cups Arborio rice

4½ cups low-sodium chicken broth

2 cups sweet peas (thawed if frozen, blanched in boiling water if fresh)

4 tablespoons unsalted butter

2 handfuls of freshly grated Parmesan cheese

Garlicky Pea Shoots (recipe follows), for serving

---

1. Preheat the oven to 400°F.

2. Place an oven-safe pot over medium heat. Add the olive oil and then the chopped shallots and sauté until soft but not browned. Add in the rice and cook it for a few minutes, stirring constantly, until the grains glisten.

3. Meanwhile, pour the broth into a separate saucepan, bring it to a boil, and immediately remove it from the heat. Add 4 cups of the hot broth to the rice mixture. Stir to combine and bring the rice pot to a boil, then cover the pot and transfer it to the oven. Cook for 20 minutes or until the liquid is mostly absorbed and the rice is tender. Remove the pot from the oven and add in the peas, butter, the remaining ½ cup of warm broth, and handfuls of Parmesan cheese. Stir everything to combine and serve topped with Garlicky Pea Shoots.

FOR BABY: The sweetness and soft texture of this risotto are perfect for baby. If you'd like, stir in finely chopped pea shoots for added nutrition.

TOMORROW'S DINNER: RISOTTO CAKES
Make a second pot of oven risotto (swap peas for any other favorite cooked veggie, like spinach, mushrooms, or asparagus), and let it sit in the refrigerator overnight. The rice will get firm and sticky. Form the rice into small patties and fry them in a large skillet coated with olive oil until crispy and browned on both sides.

GARLICKY PEA SHOOTS

serves 4

Thin, tender pea shoots are really delicious stir-fried over high heat until just wilted (not left over the heat too long to wither away). Here, I toss in some garlic, but a few grates of fresh ginger or a squirt of lemon juice is also tasty.

KIDS CAN: Kids can tear up the pea shoots with their hands or kitchen shears.

---

1 tablespoon extra virgin olive oil

1 garlic clove, minced or grated on a microplane

3 loosely packed cups pea shoots, torn into pieces

Kosher salt

---

1. Heat the oil in a medium skillet over medium-high heat. Add the minced garlic and pea shoots. Continuously toss the pea shoots with garlic until they are just wilted. Sprinkle with salt and serve on top of the risotto.

STRABERRIES WITH VANILLA SUGAR

serves 4

Dessert in the spring really means one thing—strawberries. The wild turkeys always eat the ripe berries from our plants, but happily, farm stands are not far away. If we manage to get a few pints home (without the berries being gobbled up in the backseat), I dip the strawberries in homemade vanilla sugar for a simple treat.

KIDS CAN: Children can prepare and assemble this dessert in one of two ways: either slicing the berries, dividing them among dishes, and sprinkling with vanilla sugar; or simply dipping whole berries into a bowl of vanilla sugar to coat.

| 2 cups pure cane sugar | 1 vanilla bean | 1 pint strawberries |

---

1. Pour the sugar into a large lidded glass jar. Slice the vanilla bean lengthwise and scrape the seeds into the sugar, then toss in the pod. Mix everything together. Let the jar of vanilla sugar sit on the counter for 1 to 2 weeks before using, allowing the vanilla flavor to soak into the sugar crystals.

2. To serve, simply dip whole strawberries into a small bowl of the vanilla sugar. Or, if you want something juicer, slice the berries, toss them with vanilla sugar, and set them aside at room temperature for 1 hour or until the sugar begins to dissolve and the strawberries look juicy.

FOR BABY: Babies can enjoy a pile of diced strawberries.

The Solons' Family Meal,
West Tisbury, Massachusetts

HERBY PASTA WITH MUSSELS AND LEEKS

CAESAR-ISH SALAD WITH ROSEMARY CROUTONS

RHUBARB CAKE WITH VANILLA CRÈME FRAÎCHE

shared by Gina Solon

After long, bleak months of wet, frigid weather, the days start to stretch, sometimes warming up just for a bit—just enough to cast upon us a little hope. In our family, many spring afternoons are spent outside. There is much unearthing to do from the remains of autumn and winter in our sandboxes and tree houses and gardens. And at least once a day there is a walk to our family farm. Lambs are coming at full speed now, and at any moment there could be another; you just have to peek. I love winter food—rich, substantial dishes that take hours to make—but in the spring, I am ready for brighter, crisper things. This meal is a combination of fresh and vibrant flavors, quickly assembled but still warm and comforting. Perfect for the evenings when we roll into the house with cold fingertips, smelling like the earth.

HERBY PASTA WITH MUSSELS AND LEEKS

serves 6

I usually have most of the ingredients for the pasta dish lying around, except for the mussels, which are super affordable and readily available at most fish markets.

1 pound whole-wheat spaghetti

5 tablespoons olive oil

4 leeks, white and light green parts sliced into 1-inch pieces

¾ cup dry white wine

2 pounds mussels, scrubbed and rinsed clean

3 tablespoons unsalted butter

¼ cup chopped fresh flat-leaf parsley

1 tablespoon chopped fresh thyme

1 tablespoon chopped fresh chives

Kosher salt

Red pepper flakes

1. Bring a large pot of salted water to a boil. Cook the pasta until just al dente, according to the package instructions, then drain the pasta, reserving ½ cup of the starchy cooking liquid.

2. Heat the oil in a large sauté pan over medium heat and add the leeks. Cook for 3 to 4 minutes, stirring constantly, until the leeks are slightly translucent. Add the wine, the reserved pasta water, and the mussels. Cover the pan and cook for about 5 to 6 minutes, until the mussels open. (Discard any mussels that haven't opened after cooking.)

3. Add the butter, pasta, and herbs to the pan and cook, tossing constantly, for about 1 to 2 minutes more. Season with salt and a sprinkle of red pepper flakes.

FOR BABY: As shellfish is a top allergenic food, talk to your pediatrician before experimenting with mussels. Pasta tossed with olive oil, with or without mussels, can be finely chopped for a finger food.

CAESAR-ISH SALAD WITH ROSEMARY CROUTONS

serves 4 to 6

When he was nine years old, my husband went to a restaurant where they made Caesar salad tableside, and he's been making it at home ever since. This is our toned-down, family-friendly version. The salad is easy to throw together; the littles can tear the lettuce and mix the dressing all on their own. The croutons fill the house with a toasty, rosemary scent, and often half of them are gone before they make it into the bowl.

KIDS CAN: Little hands can tear lettuce leaves for the salad and mix together the dressing.

DRESSING

⅛ cup extra virgin olive oil

2 heaping tablespoons real mayonnaise

¼ cup buttermilk

1 garlic clove, grated

2 tablespoons freshly squeezed lemon juice

Big pinch kosher salt

A few grinds freshly ground black pepper

CROUTONS

½ loaf crusty bread, cut into 1-inch cubes

Leaves from 2 sprigs fresh rosemary

4 to 5 tablespoons unsalted butter

2 large heads romaine lettuce

Freshly grated Parmesan cheese

---

1. To make the dressing, whisk together the olive oil, mayonnaise, buttermilk, garlic, lemon juice, salt, and pepper in a medium bowl. Cover and chill in the fridge for at least 15 minutes.

2. To make the croutons, preheat the oven to 400°F. Spread the bread cubes on a large, rimmed baking sheet. With a mortar and pestle, grind the rosemary until the leaves are broken down and you have kind of a paste. In a small saucepan over medium-low heat, melt the butter. Add the rosemary and swirl it around a few times to flavor the butter. Drizzle the rosemary butter over the bread cubes and toss with a spatula to coat them on all sides. Transfer the baking sheet to the oven and bake the croutons for about 10 minutes, until toasty and golden.

3. To assemble the salad, tear the romaine heads into large pieces and place them in a large salad bowl. Drizzle the lettuce with the dressing and add the croutons. Grate some Parmesan on top and toss gently with tongs.

RHUBARB CAKE WITH VANILLA CRÈME FRAÎCHE

makes one 8 by 8-inch cake

I love to make this simple cake using the abundance of rhubarb from my mother-in-law's garden. It doubles as a breakfast cake in our house, too, often inhaled on the way to the bus stop.

---

1 cup whole-wheat flour

1 cup unbleached all-purpose flour

1 teaspoon baking soda

1 teaspoon kosher salt

½ cup (1 stick) unsalted butter, at room temperature

1½ cups packed dark brown sugar

2 large eggs, at room temperature

1½ teaspoons pure vanilla extract

1 cup plain full-fat yogurt, at room temperature

3 to 4 stalks fresh rhubarb, trimmed and cut into 1-inch pieces

1 tablespoon grated fresh gingerroot

VANILLA CRÈME FRAÎCHE

Seeds from 1 vanilla bean

One 8-ounce container crème fraîche

2 tablespoons confectioners' sugar

---

1. Grease an 8 by 8-inch baking dish and preheat the oven to 350°F.

2. In a large bowl, stir together the flours, baking soda, and salt. In the bowl of an electric mixer fitted with the paddle attachment, cream together the butter and sugar. Add the eggs and vanilla, beat well to combine, then alternate between the flour mixture and the yogurt, adding a little at a time and beating well between additions. When all the flour and yogurt has been incorporated, fold in the rhubarb and ginger with a wooden spoon or rubber spatula.

3. Pour the batter into the prepared baking dish and bake for about 55 minutes or until a knife inserted in the center comes out clean.

4. To make the crème fraîche topping, mix together all the ingredients in a small bowl. Cover and refrigerate for at least 15 minutes or until chilled. Top the cake slices with dollops of the crème fraîche.

FOR BABY: Rhubarb cake can be crumbled into bits for a special treat.

A Savory (and Very Green) Pie

SKILLET SPINACH PIE

PUFFED BROWN RICE TREATS

I grew up in a suburb of Boston. My hometown looks a lot different now than it did thirty years ago. Now, Main Street is lined with bustling restaurants, upscale stores, and fancy wine shops. Back in the day, we made our way between an ice cream shop, movie rental store, and Greek restaurant. This neighborhood Greek restaurant is where our family would go for a night out. I first saw moussaka, tasted egg-lemon soup, and bit into baklava sitting around its white-clothed tables. My order was always a slice of spinach pie, a dish I continue to love today. This meal is a simple, home-cooked version of the Greek classic, paired with my twist on another classic, crispy rice treats.

SKILLET SPINACH PIE

serves 8

Foolproof skillet meals are hard to beat, and this one is just as impressive as it is delicious. Don't be intimidated by the phyllo dough—an imperfect top will only result in more crisp edges. I often grill up a few local pork sausages to serve alongside this vegetable pie, but a big slice on its own is perfectly good, too.

KIDS CAN: Kids can wrap the cooked spinach in kitchen towels and squeeze out the moisture.

---

30 ounces frozen spinach, thawed

5 tablespoons unsalted butter

1 small yellow onion, minced

2 cups whole-milk ricotta cheese

4 large eggs, lightly beaten

⅓ cup crumbled feta cheese

3 tablespoons chopped fresh dill

Juice of 1 lemon

1 teaspoon kosher salt

Freshly ground black pepper

6 sheets frozen phyllo dough, thawed

---

1. Preheat the oven to 375°F.

2. Place the spinach in the center of a clean kitchen towel, then fold up the edges and squeeze out as much moisture as you can.

3. In a 10-inch cast iron (or other ovenproof) skillet, melt the butter over medium heat. Transfer 2 tablespoons of melted butter to a small bowl. Add the minced onion to the skillet and cook until softened, about 5 minutes. Turn off the heat and let the pan cool slightly, then stir in the spinach, ricotta, eggs, feta, dill, lemon juice, salt, and a few grinds of pepper.

4. Lay the first sheet of phyllo dough over the spinach-ricotta mixture in the skillet and brush the top with some of the reserved melted butter. One at a time, layer on the remaining five sheets, brushing each with butter. Rotate and scrunch each sheet slightly so the edges are offset and the top is ruffled. Transfer the pie to the oven and bake until golden brown and heated through, about 35 minutes.

FOR BABY: Spinach tends to be stringy, so whiz a serving of pie in a food processor to break up any long strands.

TOMORROW'S DINNER: This recipe makes a big pan of spinach pie, plenty for leftovers. Serve a quick Greek egg-lemon soup or pan of lamb meatballs with the leftovers.

PUFFED BROWN RICE TREATS

makes about 16 treats

If the kids are eager to help in the kitchen, we often choose to make these treats for dessert. The recipe can be completed by little helpers, start to finish, and takes only a few minutes to get from mixing bowl to mouth. This recipe makes a slightly sweet treat. If you like a stronger dose of sweetness, add in another tablespoon of maple syrup. Similarly, the treats are soft and squishy at first (they harden up on the counter). If you want a firm, crisp treat from the start, add in a bit more of the sticky stuff (brown rice syrup and nut butter).

---

5 cups puffed brown rice cereal

1 teaspoon coconut oil, melted

1 cup brown rice syrup

2 tablespoons almond butter (or any nut or seed butter)

2 tablespoons pure maple syrup

2 teaspoons pure vanilla extract

---

1. Pour the cereal into a large mixing bowl.

2. Place the coconut oil in a saucepan over medium-high heat. Add in the rice syrup, almond butter, and maple syrup. Stir to combine and heat until bubbles form. Let the mixture boil for 5 minutes, then immediately turn off the heat and stir in the vanilla extract.

3. Pour the syrup into the bowl with the cereal and mix well. Scrape the mixture into an 8 by 8-inch pan. With slightly wet hands, press the mixture flat. Let it cool to room temperature, then slice it into squares and serve. If your eaters are eager, you can dig in right away, but the bars will be lose. Leftover treats can be stored in an airtight container at room temperature for up to 1 week.

FOR BABY: If your baby is comfortable with nuts, pull a rice treat apart into small grains of finger food. If you are avoiding nuts, swap the almond butter for a seed butter instead.